The Island Self

Poems by Howard Blake

THE ISLAND SELF

Edited & with an Introduction by

ROBERT KENT

Foreword by

AUSTIN WARREN

David R. Godine

Two thousand five hundred copies of this book have been printed at the Press of David R. Godine in Brookline, Mass. It was designed by Carol Shloss and set in Monotype Perpetua by A. Colish, Inc. of Mt. Vernon, N.Y. The paper is a specially made Almanac Text Gray Laid. The edition was bound by A. Horowitz & Son.

DAVID R. GODINE PUBLISHER
BOSTON, MASSACHUSETTS

LCC 72-91755
ISBN 0-87923-066-5

Acknowledgment is made to Brown University for permission to use the manuscripts of Howard Blake in the Harris Collection of American Poetry and Plays, Brown University Library.

The drawing on the jacket and frontispiece was made by Jack Coughlin.

CONTENTS

THESE QUESTIONS FOR BALANCE
1936-(1943)

LAST POEMS

1942-

FOREWORD

I FIRST MET Howard Blake in 1931. One of the young women I taught at Boston University had written a character sketch of Poe, which included reference to her knowing a modern analogue. I asked to meet him. Blake accepted the invitation: a thin and very pale seventeen-year-old, carefully dressed in a dark blue suit with white shirt and black tie. He was ceremonious of manner and precise of diction. It was not difficult to imagine him a poet.

He told the story of his earlier life in installments. To one of my conservative rearing, his tale sounded so fantastic and melodramatic that I suspended my judgment of its accuracy; but, after years of hearing fragments of the story in differing contexts, I could not doubt its essential truth. His grandparents on both sides came from the Massachusetts south of Boston – chiefly from Attleboro: solid, respectable Yankee Protestants. With his parents, rebellion and decadence – rise and decline – entered the family. His father, a traveling salesman, had made a fabulous salary; and the Blakes lived in what Howard remembered as high style – a style at least much above that of their Wollaston neighbors. There was a rose garden, and a part-time gardener, with whose little son Howard, perhaps rather patronizingly, played. He sang in the boys' choir at St. Chrysostom's Episcopal Church, and was, I think, confirmed.

This life came to an end when Blake was about ten. His mother, the second Mrs. Blake, had various affairs and finally ran away with a man already married. His father was found to be supporting several additional wives on his route. He contracted syphilis; then went insane; then died.

For some years after the breakup of the family, the boy was supported by a well-to-do uncle, who wanted to make a businessman out of him. He was sent to live with a family in Lexington, where he attended the public school for a few years; then for a year to a private day school in

BY AUSTIN WARREN

Hartford. With not more than a year or two of secondary school, his formal education ended. His uncle found him some kind of menial job in Boston which, after a few months, he gave up; whereupon his uncle cast him off.

There followed a period when he was without steady support. For a time, a classics master at a country day school provided for him; then a young man from Kansas, who came to Boston with a copy of Emerson as his guide, shared a room. The widow of an Episcopal priest, a poetess and the mother of an early dead Harvard poet, was hospitable. Another benefactor was a Harvard man, the son of a Newbury Street physician, who lived (Boston fashion) on an allowance from his family, had traveled much in the Orient, and had adopted Buddhism — a gentleman of little intellect but of fine taste, urbanity, and self-knowledge.

None of his friends doubted Blake's special quality, indeed, distinction: he was not merely intelligent, appealing, touching, but, in the German or Romantic sense of the word, a genius. He combined delicacy of perception with boldness of judgment, and a mental agility of response with a vigor of argumentation; he showed self-will, determination, even obstinacy in holding his own. He had the assurance of desperation. The traumatic early life (of which he spoke only at the beginning of our friendship) had precociously defined both self and vocation.

None of these friends would have doubted that this young poet deserved support; but none could manage it. For my part, I was a professor of English, one of whose special fields was poetry; and I earned my livelihood teaching the works of the dead poets. I felt that I had a responsibility to provide for a living poet in need, such a real and promising poet as, after a few months of acquaintance, I judged him to be; and so I became, in a modest way, a patron of poetry, aided in later years by other such patrons.

The resumption of his formal education seemed impracticable, almost irrelevant; and during the next four or five years, until Blake was in his early twenties, he was half an autodidact, half privately tutored. His friends irregularly taught him, either in 'lessons' or in conversation, whatever they knew and cared about: Latin, German, Chinese and Japanese art, philosophy (one close friend, a Harvard graduate student, admired Leibniz, Santayana, and Whitehead, and did his best to impart their essences). With another friend he studied voice production; by yet another he was coached in the *Lieder* of Schubert and Wolf, which he sang well, being possessed of both a good baritone and musical intelligence.

I set him to reading the prose of the seventeenth and eighteenth centuries, especially Sir Thomas Browne and Dr. Johnson. Unlike my college students, Blake read straight through the *Lives of the Poets*, the minors as well as the majors, Akenside and Dyer as well as Pope; and he delighted in the sombre wisdom and stylistic rigidity of *Rasselas*. From Browne and Johnson he learned his syntax.

When I met him, he had already been writing poetry for at least two years, the kind of poetry his elderly literary friends admired – rondeaux, villanelles, sonnets – poems in 'strict' forms as well as thin, musical, lyrical verse derivative from the English and American poets of the nineties. It was I, I think, who introduced him to the then moderns, Eliot, the Stevens of *Harmonium*, Hart Crane – and later Father Hopkins – as well as to my favorite 'metaphysical' poets. Together we read and analyzed the moderns: it was the first serious close exegesis of poetry I had ever done; and at this the young poet was probably the real guide and teacher.

His analysis was for his own purposes. Almost immediately he rejected his earlier work as 'juvenilia.' He began to imitate Eliot and Stevens, once at least showing me a poem he referred to as Eliotic. The textural resemblance seemed far from marked. Blake's chief debt to Eliot is the allusive method; but he does not quote Eliot's quotations: he ranged widely outside the moderns and the 'metaphysicals'; and Diogenes Laertius and William Dunbar and the *Confessions* of St. Augustine and Crashaw and Waller, all quoted or alluded to in the *Prolegomena*, he had really read.

The general principles and methods of Blake's poetry were on the whole conscious, and were carried out with almost too much system in his revisions. He was not and did not want to be a 'lyrical' poet – a writer of songs or musical poetry – any more than he wanted to write out of untranslated, unrefracted experience: his lyric must be 'on other terms.' He wanted to write some kind of short-hand, compressed, abridged, modern kind of poem, juxtaposing the past and the present, the recondite and the popular – Cimarosa and 'Joe Praz.'

Despite occasional showy alliterative lines like 'That worms should wallow where wren willow was,' he did not desire euphony. Nor did he want lines that flowed. Flowing lines involve plenty of unstressed syllables and articles; Blake avoided the definite article, for he wanted every syllable to tell. A poem should be all poetry: he still held to the Eliot of *Waste Land* as against the Eliot of *Four Quartets*.

So my young friend went on reading, revising, his intelligence ever operative – his compulsion, poetry. And he had Boston for his world. He was a youth and then a man of the large city. As a boy he had spent the summer with his family on the Cape; and he returned to the Cape to live for two years in the fifties. In the thirties he took short vacations at Provincetown. He had a proper love of the ocean (not, in his poems, a mere archetype): he was an excellent swimmer. Though he liked short visits to the New England countryside, he would not long have been contented anywhere except in the city. He needed sidewalks, bars – in which not only to drink but to encounter. He needed secondhand book shops and art shops, the general gamut from the refined and the aristocratic to the coarse and the crude, which only the city gives – also its anonymity and the freedom of hours, to live one's own schedule.

This creative period, which began in 1932, went on for something between five and ten years. In 1937 it seemed to his friends that Blake, whose book had been published the year before, should now have the best equivalent of a university education – a year in Europe, the Grand Tour. This *annus mirabilis* occurred. He visited the museums. He met literary men: in England, both Eliot and Dr. Leavis received him cordially. But chiefly this was a year of seeing, feeling, and being: of sensibility.

He returned to Boston at the height of his striking good looks and intellectual powers, and began planning a second book, never to be published in his lifetime.

★   ★   ★

The Blake of the forties and fifties, when I saw him on my summer visits to Boston, was, I judge, far less of a reader than he used to be; and his reading was far less literary, though, despite a taste formed by the thirties, he kept up to some degree with current poetry. He was more likely to be reading current psychiatry, in which he took a keen interest, or anthropology – whether Margaret Mead or Robert Graves' *The White Goddess*.

He never entirely stopped writing, though he ceased to think of publishing. On almost every visit I paid, he would, as it neared its close, take out some manuscripts and read aloud to me, in his sonorous voice – chiefly, I remember, from that impressive poem,' He Thought to Utter Ocean,' or from a sequence of poems derived from the family genealogy he was then systematically exploring, not only through printed records but through visits to family graveyards south of Boston. These manuscripts I was not permitted to see: they were still in process, and revised in the act of reading. But the attempt to break through into some freer mode of writing than the 'Blake style' appeared so successful that I was disappointed by the fragmentary state of what survived. I would, upon my visits, ever urge him to publish; and he would ever refuse on the ground that the poems were still under revision. In fact, publication only became possible when, after Blake's death, the immediate family gave me his manuscripts.

Presumably Blake's perfectionism was one cause of his failure to publish. Presumably the essentially solipsistic nature of his metaphysics, the absence, at any period, of any faith or hope in religion (he was the determined foe of the Church), or in any at once practical and ultimately worthy political reform, was another. Art (primarily, but not exclusively, poetry) and personal relationships – at which he was an adept – had to provide all the reason for living. The chief cause, however, was probably the isolated position in which he found himself, in the last twenty and, especially, the last ten years, even in Boston (the only city outside London I can imagine his living in), and even though that isolation was privately, personally mitigated in his last years by a sustaining marriage and the much desired birth of a son and the adoption of another

– by the creation of 'family.' Like most literary men, he needed not only steadying personal attachments but a professional ambience – other poets with whom to talk, others to whom mattered those pursuits and goals which are central to a literary *elite* – that kind of relatively impersonal sustainment.

Though Blake was acquainted with a considerable number of his literary contemporaries, some well known, most of them not, he had but one frequent companion and real friend among them, John Brooks Wheelwright, the Harvard poet, of Beacon Street, Boston. For some five years, till his sudden death in 1940, Wheelwright, nearly a generation older, who, like Blake, had no stated occupation other than that of poet, took a fellow-poet's and something like an elder-brother's interest in him. After the fashion of their kind, the two read their poems aloud to each other, criticized each other's work, made suggestions for revision. Jack used to urge Howard to loosen up his work by 'putting in some mashed potato'; he also accepted Blake's suggestions for improved – presumably stiffened or thickened – lines to insert in his own poems. Jack took Howard with him to the short-lived clubs of 'bards' he was always assembling, to the politically liberal Cambridge Poetry Forum, and to Mrs. Fiske Warren's conservative New England Poetry Society (131 Mt. Vernon Place), at the meetings of which the two intellectual and literary mavericks were the only ones to utter forthright criticisms – sometimes denunciations – of their elderly women fellow-members.

Wheelwright's death left Blake without the talk of a fellow poet. Then in 1941, Eleanor, his sister and senior by five years, who in recent years had shared an apartment with him, married me and left Boston for Iowa City. A year after our marriage, she showed the first signs of the multiple sclerosis from which, four years later, she died. The relation between brother and sister had been very close. She had been an ally and protector since his boyhood. They were united not only by painful shared memories but also, as I learned, by laughter, fun, nonsense, gaiety. How great was his dependence the brother recognized only after her departure – or departures. First followed prolonged, grief and then a mysterious illness, seemingly some kind of paralysis. His mental acuity and vigor remained; but his physical movements were more and more restricted. Yet to the end he delighted in entertaining; and an evening at the Blake apartment on Huntington Avenue was intellectually exciting.

That Howard Blake never sought a post as writer-in-residence or teacher of writing at some university is a matter of some regret to me. For such a post he was in many ways suited: he was an excellent practical critic; he had charm and intensity; he was clearly understood and liked by the student writers whom he met during his visits to Iowa and Michigan. Some attachment to an institution might well have given a very different and more productive turn to his later years. And yet, from first to last, his independence, his 'courage to be,' his refusal to be intimidated by the authority of name or status, were among the virtues I respected him for – those non-academic virtues hard to reconcile with the real other values of an educational establishment.

In our present period of confessional verse, Blake's poetry is outmoded: so 'made,' so 'written.' Yet there is a violence of feeling, a rage, behind it which exists in tension with the witty, allusive, and contrived 'precious' surface: this felt violence, the rage behind the order, is perhaps its most marked quality. In his character there existed this same tension between surface and substance: the code of manners and speech of a gentleman, and deep capacities for hate, anger, love, loyal friendship, great sympathy and tenderness, all expressed with little of the celebrated New England reserve.

The traits of my friend which I most admired were his sometimes terrifying integrity and his self-definition. He would not compromise; he would not equivocate. In contrast to most people, he was clear about his appetites and his ambitions. He knew what he wanted; and this rather rare virtue gave him power and authority. With these masculine traits of defined goals and standards he combined others; he possessed, even in his youth, much subtlety and flexibility of adjustment to persons and situations: from his fixed point of view, he spoke to the person immediately with him and to the immediate occasion or situation they shared.

In the records of Mt. Auburn cemetery, the entry for Howard Blake reports 'Usual occupation: Poet.' The epitaph is altogether appropriate

Jeffers, Aiken, Robinson, and others now seem less than necessary, the 'Thoughts,' like the letter, betray a young man ready to participate in a great action: the one, whole, and continuous epic of literature.

Two 'Thoughts' are worth noting here.

The nineteenth-century and the present day have named the lyrical in poetry as the one thing needful: to avoid the trite; to sustain the power of each line, in relation, not to other lines, but to itself, has been the formulated doctrine of modern poets. Perhaps the Zeitgeist of modernity has its nearest analogue in the age of Donne, but we must remember that from his century rose a Milton. Today's poets may be too intelligent to be epic poets; they may find difficulty, defeat when confronted with the need to confine mankind to some outlined theory or idea – the necessary order for epic composition. Perhaps, from these ashes, some poet with the required limitations will rise.

(XLIII, 190)

The 'ranting' writer is still too 'intelligent' to produce less than the best in him – whatever the *Zeitgeist* – yet

Mr. Eliot's subjective approach to the epic (what he would consider, and perhaps he is right, the only possible form of composition for this age) and Hart Crane's attempt for a more objective achievement, are arresting instances of current impotence. Mr. Eliot's nice writing and Hart Crane's broad splashes have this in common: both are subjective; intent (consciously in Mr. Eliot's case, I believe, unconsciously in Hart Crane's) on words, not sections; lacking any positive, determined, ruling conception of life (a belief which automatically excludes exceptions); lacking in universality.

(XLIII, 194)

A very 'positive, determined, ruling conception of' art indeed. Surely there is truth in these autocratic strictures; surely as much truth in recognition as in intuition.

Blake was simply too close, in time and in kind, to both Eliot and Crane. Old before his time, he did sense problems 'in common'; but

18

the ruins of his own epic lie somewhere between the 'nice writing' of Eliot's 'Prufrock' and the 'broad splashes' of Crane's *Bridge*: first to last Blake is consciously and unconsciously intent on words, intense but insulated. I shall develop this estimate later.

But Blake's prose is instructive, for all its parenthetical play. At twenty-one he had ready a number of essential tricks and restraints; and while it seems to me that he learned his prejudices, through Eliot, from Dryden, Dr. Johnson, and Coleridge, I sense also an independent mind like Eliot's. The critic engages 'thoughts,' as almost necessary acts of the imagination; he dares to make metaphors. He is not an academic drudge, carefully scouring the dull black letter of books. And Blake's prose improved. The reviews for *Poetry* are swift, sure in their artful lack of transition, penetrating, wise. Unfortunately, they treat well-forgotten books. The 'Thoughts,' however, pertain: and read against Crane's short and justly admired manifesto, 'Modern Poetry' (1930), Blake's thoughts on the subject are stimulating.

Blake had friends: poets dead and gone whom he revived and was revived by; his sister Eleanor; a living (though surrogate) family of Bostonians, literary and artistic; common and cultivated bedfellows; benefactors. But the long decades from 1940 to 1960 were largely waste. His early and formative circle, which included Austin Warren and the poet John Brooks Wheelwright, dissolved. Friends died or married or moved away. Publication stopped. Although he married and had a son, Blake never had gainful employment or institutional attachment. The death of his sister, in 1946, and the haunted 'Sestina to Memory As Eleanor Blake Warren' mark the beginning of the end.

'They died on me,' he used to say; and to Austin Warren's essay on Emily Dickinson (1957) he contributed these knowing remarks: 'How angry we feel when one towards whom we had felt, or protested we did, dies on us. He or she has up and left us. Ashamed of anger towards the ''loved dead'' – or those who have separated from us, one denies the feeling. Emily's ''white election'' is not wholly devoid of moral blackmail, consequent guilts – rich pasture for poetry.'

*　　*　　*

Such pastures – more accurately, the wilds of Howard Blake's poetry – are civilized by a number of deaths and denials. Blake took his attachments selfishly, and sought restitution for loss – in verse. Yet he shunned easy monumentality, the simpler colonnades and architraves of grief, adorned by discreet friezes of the identifiable loved. His work is mannerist – bold and precious, swept back and stubborn, cunning, even brutal. He was, I am told, most mannerly – very presentable, learned and sure of speech, able among all books and classes, tastes and sexes. He must have been a violent man within. The bald denials, the 'musts' of his poems, suggest the opposite of 'moral blackmail': if Blake's poems *do* anything, they exploit anger, without shame or sin. The poet means to trip death, and to make love live.

His only book was published in Boston, early in 1936. He called it *Prolegomena to Any Future Poetry* and, lest a reader mistake its forbidding title, he took care to announce 'the restricted obvious' in a preface: 'Any first book of verse is prolegomena to any other verse conceived, at some future time, by the same writer. On the other hand, it may mean what, in reality, every man, when he publishes a collection of his verse, means – that all poetry in the future will be, or should be, written in such wise as to indicate that its author had read, and profited from reading, this collection.' The paragraphs that follow, with their terribly sane assessment of the modern poet and his problems, owe much to T. S. Eliot. More tellingly, they show in their urgent maturity how genius understands everything but its own madness.

One of the best poems of the *Prolegomena* is entitled 'Argent Solipsism.' It first appeared in *Poetry*, in October 1935. (The one typescript that survives, a carbon copy of an earlier version, is dated 19 November 1934 – when Blake was still twenty years old.) A sentence in the 'Thoughts on Modern Poetry' is of particular moment in the reading of it: 'This nineteenth-century, this age of romanticists, also espoused the exploitation of personality, laying the foundations for much of the current solipsistic verse.' (XLIII, 194-5) If the 'Solipsism' succeeds, it is because Blake's words invite not exploitation of, but escape from, personality. Straight Eliot doctrine – but with an important twist.

The speaker of 'Argent Solipsism,' an objectified self, sings his own defense; we are not asked to characterize him – as we can, say, Prufrock. The listener – both the particularized 'you' and the more general audience – is the one exploited. His is the 'donored' personality. Or to put it more closely: 'It is *you* who are intent and withholding, trapped by meaning, in a hope of pretty sounds. *My* words affirm real and imagined worlds, you *and* me, wind and ornament, and only these "pontiff syllables" can mean what I am.' Stated, the solipsism isn't very cosy; as poetry it is passionate and, to my eyes, dazzling.

Where does such silver selfhood come from? What gives it value? I think one important donor is Catullus. Some phrases seem to have been appropriated – not really paraphrased, but taken and *set* to immediate advantage. For example, 'So quiet as the ether between stars' (line 7) recalls *aut quam sidera multa, cum tacet nox* (VII, 7), 'as many as are stars, when night is quiet,' from the early sequence to Lesbia. Or, 'a pain that seeps through every vein' (line 9) and 'sounds of winds that slide / With pointless whimpers' (lines 11-12) suggest Catullus LI, the superb translation from Sappho. A case for Catullus could be made by further noting that, in the *Prolegomena*, 'Argent Solipsism' is preceded by a poem entitled 'Vivimus Quod Vivimus' and followed by 'Night Stand,' a sly interpolation to Catullus VI, which incorporates lines 13-14 of the Latin. But more, it is the Catullan spirit – chaste and profane, fastidious and gross – that informs a number of Blake's early poems. And the classical sound, with its resonance and wide orchestral resources, finds a new voice in Blake: not a senseless music, but a measured and highly individualized phrase.

There are other donors: Keats and Eliot. In particular, 'Keen Fitful Gusts' and J. Alfred Prufrock's 'Love Song.' The circumstances of Keats's sonnet – his long cold walk from Hampstead, after an evening at Leigh Hunt's – seem to have found a modern equivalent. (It may be worth remembering that Blake, in the letter quoted above, disallowed his becoming another Hunt.) I don't think it too far afield to suggest that Blake's very imagery penetrates Keats's: the stars, the lamps, the colors silver and green, the 'pointless whimpers through garrets glazed with dust' (line 12) *vs.* 'fitful gusts … whisp'ring here and there / Among the bushes half leafless, and dry' (the opening lines of the Keats). Of course, with 'Prufrock,' the scene has become urban: it is not Keats's 'feel I little … of those silver lamps that burn on high' (lines 5-8), but 'Never to tread the cobbles under lamps / Shedding their perpendicular inane' (lines 20-21). Yet the affirmation is Keats's – rid of romantic 'damask' and 'curls.' And perhaps the whole last stanza of 'Argent Solipsism' is Blake's answer to Eliot's quailed spokesman: he who had vowed not 'to turn teacups.' The poem is spoken in the first person – who else would know what (I am) to say? – and like good lyric utterance it is not really personal, not an *expression* of personality.

Wallace Stevens had something to do with 'Argent Solipsism.' The title and its idea, the *mots justes* of 'callower crescendos,' 'blue paradigms,' and 'pontiff syllables,' could well have come from the maker of *Harmonium.* Blake's debt to Stevens is consciously celebrated in 'These Questions for Balance,' a poem begun in the year of the *Prolegomena* but not published until 1943, when it appeared in *Accent.* The six autobiographical 'Questions,' Blake's search for his own *Ideas of Order,* end in a garish, twilit abstract:

> *The questions, the balance, O Harmodius,*
> *(The dark is cocktail to concupiscence*
> *And science that freeze taut fingers with ice glare)*
> *Have made a twilight of insatiate sense,*
> *Have given silence audience, have inscribed*
> *Aloof arkana on chameleon air.*

Silence *was* given audience: 'These Questions for Balance' was to be Blake's last publication. Seventeen long years out of print, of sporadic composition, remained to him.

★   ★   ★

Perhaps it is time to raise those questions that readers of a new collection of unknown poems would naturally ask, *for balance.* What effect, if any, have the poems of Howard Blake on the twentieth-century American canon? – and why this late introduction of them? Just what, precisely, is Blake's relation to Eliot, to Stevens and Crane? Can one say that, having read Blake, one knows more about the greater poets? Why did Blake stop writing? – or was he simply a *Wunderkind*? How, finally, do the poems of Howard Blake hold up? Posterity may continue to ask the last and most important of these questions; I should like to try a few brief and necessarily tentative answers.

The ancestor of American romantic poetry of the twentieth century is John Keats; and the ancient question Keats raises in the 'Nightingale,' 'Do I wake or sleep?' – the question tempered by Arnold, and occasionally by Tennyson, to modern unhappiness – is the 'overwhelming question' that disturbs Prufrock, 'Till human voices wake us, and we drown.' To Arnold, to Eliot, it is the question of Will and its corollary, Paralysis, in a ruined world. To the poet who is implicated, it means both the literal senses and the literary sensibility. Who are *you*, it rudely forces; what can *you* do, now? Honestly asked, courageously posed, and skilfully dramatized, it has become a major subject of modern poetry, from 'Lines Written in Kensington Gardens' to 'The Quaker Graveyard in Nantucket.' And it is a question bound by convention, for since 'Dover Beach' it has become a mode: however actually aware the poet is of his times, he cannot meditate the Thankless Muse in odes unconscious of 'Eternal passion! / Eternal pain!'; or like Gerontion he must 'Think now' in elegies of 'reconsidered passion.'

Blake's poems, it seems to me, are radically subject to the will. An acknowledged paralysis sets in, in poem after poem, whatever their ostensible object: whether in the cold pastoral of the early lyrics – 'gulls ... with shattered shriek' ('Overtones'), 'fevered thinking ... in brittle notes' and 'sleeping throats ... like prisoned silver birds' ('Analyse des Amants'), 'With acid undulate unrest ... With gaunt quiescence' ('Rebellion') – or in the word within a word of the late meditations – 'Eternal solid in a frozen hour,' 'that stuttering / Of silence, oak, torn air' ('Emergency'), 'Unspoken though inherent plan' ('Habe Ja Doch Nichts Begangen'), 'Deaf to the quiet many things suggest' ('10 September 1950. 4 AM'), 'The agony of dead thing in the bone' ('He

Thought to Utter Ocean'). Blake nourishes 'That wild, unquench'd, deep-sunken, old-world pain' of Arnold's 'Philomela,' not the 'golden grin' of Eliot's 'Sweeney.'

Fame at the expense of nobility, art at the expense of life, wisdom at the expense of innocence – these are problems that have always bothered poets, in some degree. Excessive (or obsessive) concern for self, however, can mean no poetry; for without a subject more worthy, more vital, more unpremeditated than his aging self, the poet has less and less to do. With a few remarkable exceptions – occasions when the object of his efforts was felt worthy – Blake had little to say after his twenty-third year. By 1938 his *Prolegomena* was two years old; his major poem, the 'Questions,' was well underway (he had first called it 'The View at Twenty-Two' – i.e., 1936); he had written an extraordinary sequence of poems in Europe (which I will take up shortly); and he had returned to Boston for twenty-three years of unproductive melancholia. Like the terrible words *Any Future* in the title of his *Prolegomena*, the poem 'On His Being Arrived at the Age of Twenty-Three' – so sternly promising a moment for its great predecessor, John Milton – seems almost bent on denying to Howard Milton Blake the prospect of maturity:

> *To be another year, another ell*
> *On aimless architecture, impertinent*
> *To brain and shorn of all the still heart's point;*
> *Willing to sing, enamored quite to please,*
> *Tonight immense, some hours to distil*
> *In murmurs toward an undistinguished sea,*
> *Leaving the boy's specific continent,*
> *Bleached by the enervation of idea.*

Every poet is in search of an epic, a wholeness of time and world and self. A great poet like Stevens is able to turn a state of mind – say, disillusionment – to advantage: to identify the pain, to search its cause and course through a discovery of words, and to isolate the moment long enough to give it life and perhaps a name. The end of this process is art; and the epic dimension of this art – whatever formal mode the poet, or his subject, chooses – is its lifelikeness. One reads poem after poem by Stevens, book after book, responding continually to the named life of a unified mind. *Prolegomena to Any Future Poetry* sets forth the 'eclogues,' the select pieces of a young poet. One poem follows, interpenetrates, another; the last poems in the book, longer and more relaxed, seem to grow naturally out of the first short tense ones. Before he left in April 1937 for his *Wanderjahr*, Blake had achieved a stride: an unrhymed, measured and sectioned (not really stanzaed) poem of about thirty lines. 'Argent Solipsism' is premonitory; the six 'Questions for Balance' are at the mode's exhausted end. Greater occasions – and their independent ends – were to follow, but Blake never again hit or sustained such a stride.

If melancholy and a wilful subjection to the limits of a self-worn mode marked Blake early, I would nonetheless suggest that the poems deserve more than a passing tribute. Read against Crane's *White Buildings*, which ends in that magnificent 'wink of eternity,' the six 'Voyages,' Blake's *Prolegomena* and 'Six Questions' are rawer, more daring, and free of careless rapture and sentimentality. Blake lacks Crane's full-bodied lightness – and that is why, perhaps, he will be taken less seriously – but he has greater energy. His poems do not aspire to the condition of music; he was attracted to the 'mighty line.' His poetry seeks – and, where it is best, finds – a well-spoken phrase to comprehend his mind. For rendered *subject*, though, I doubt that any of the early poems can hold up against 'Black Tambourine' or 'Voyages II.'

For a slim volume of six hundred copies, *Prolegomena to Any Future Poetry* had a widely attentive press. Donald Davidson, in the *Southern Review*, touched a live nerve: 'the modern thing: ... Mr. Blake has affiliations with Eliot and Hart Crane, but he seems less interested than they in what the whole poem does with an idea or mood; he wants to dig into the inside works and see what goes on or what can be made to go on.' In reviews and testimonials, Merrill Moore, John Holmes, David

Cornel DeJong, and others also responded to 'what can be made to go on': they emphasized the poet's demands and the reader's rewards, deferring the question, Would this talent, this 'prodigious technical brilliance' (*New York Herald Tribune*), persist? It was an interesting moment, 1936. First books by American poets who would persist were very few: Richard Eberhart's *Reading the Spirit* and Robert Penn Warren's *Thirty-six Poems* are the only ones of note. (Both men were ten years older than Blake.) But books by established poets were considerable: Frost's *A Further Range*, Sandburg's *The People, Yes*, Eliot's *Burnt Norton*, Cummings's *1/20*, Tate's *The Mediterranean and Other Poems*. And important books had appeared the year before: Stevens's *Ideas of Order*, Bishop's *Minute Particulars*, Williams's *An Early Martyr and Other Poems*, Jeffers's *Solstice*, and Marianne Moore's *Selected Poems*. Without a second collection, and without more critical attention, Blake was bound to fall into obscurity by the forties, when his immediate contemporaries began to establish themselves.

Of the poets Blake knew, two, both older men, achieved and held some recognition: Winfield Townley Scott, associated with the *Providence Journal* and with *Smoke*, a little magazine in which four of Blake's poems appeared; and John Brooks Wheelwright, Blake's close professional associate, whose death in 1940 was a serious personal loss, remembered in the poem 'Notes for an Elegy.' As for the poets who were born on the eve of the First World War and who found themselves in 'perilous balance' with the Second, Blake knew none of them. History may yet name this generation – Schwartz, Shapiro, Blake, Jarrell, Berryman – the truly 'lost'; poets who dug too far 'into the inside works' and who tried to make too much 'go on.' (Lowell, slightly younger, may also be included.) But Blake's relation to Eliot, Stevens, and Crane, a closer relation than to his immediate contemporaries, is more relevant; and I suspect that the poems of this volume – the reprinted 'Questions,' particularly, and the later poems that draw into his mode the sexuality of his European experience – will occasion some re-estimation of romantic poetry in our century.

The poems that came out of nine months in European capitals and spas are sensual, specifically homosexual. I know of no other poems like them. They follow as closely on the heels of living and spending as poems of hypersexuality are ever likely to – and still be poetry, sufficiently free of personality. They are intensely physical poems, bound by a hard mentality: what losses or gains in love they tell are but cousin to the word sought, the phrase tried, the idea realized. The manuscripts reflect very few changes or revisions, and it is clear from a marginal note, written some time in the early forties, that, of the European poems, Blake intended to include only two – of the least defined sexually – in a proposed new book. That book was never finished; only one poem was finally published, in *American Prefaces*, 1940.

Two poems of the sequence – one written at the beginning of a love affair (dated Paris, 9 September 1937) and another near the end of Blake's stay in Europe (dated 14 December) – are especially noteworthy. The first, 'Is There a Word to Burst the Subtle Skin,' is a loose sonnet, with only three definite rhymes and a casually final couplet; the second, 'The Expectation,' is written in thirteen lines of deliberate blank verse. Both pose questions – a number of the European poems begin with the question 'Is there ... ?' – and the image of the scalpel and the theme of expectation are common to both.

In asking the first and perhaps most relevant question, What sort of poetry is this?, one is forced to admit obstacles. What does one do when suddenly confronted with 'Your expectant balls'? And if one knows where to look for comparison – and I know of no printed place – how does one measure the effect? Whatever the sexual experience of the reader, real or imagined, the shock is there. Is one to say, 'This was not meant to be published,' or, if this is poetry of a high order, and I think it is, is one to change one's notion of American literature? In the second poem, to my mind the more powerful, is the portent which comes to a troubled intelligence in what seems to be a Turkish bath admissible? Are the words, 'Here I am, this need needs remedy,' haunted and haunting as they are, inevitable? I leave these questions unanswered, not out of any squeamishness but because I simply don't know. I know only that I have had to accommodate the poems to my experience; that a line such as 'Eager redemption castrate in a mist' is wild and strange – and unforgettable. I accept the genuineness of these poems, and I admire their art.

*   *   *

Something remains to be said of Howard Blake's last works, of his artistry in general, and of my editing of his poems. Working with the manuscripts, which came to me in a jumble, I was soon aware of the poet's habits. He always *saw through* a version or revision: he was deliberate and orderly. Some poems are overwrought: most of these he abandoned or never considered publishing. With a few exceptions I have taken the latest version of Blake's unpublished work for my edition. My decisions on exceptions and my arrival at the latest versions should have some comment. I should also mention the juvenilia, the translations, and the unfinished poems that I have excluded.

An early, brilliant poem, overwritten and abandoned, is an Italian sonnet called 'Overtones.' I have chosen to begin the book with it – that is, with the first version. I regard the second and third versions as inferior. (My choice is at least half borne out by the poet: having carried the poem through three versions, Blake chose not to include it in the *Prolegomena*.) I give the unprinted third version below, with changes in roman:

> *While* he was vigilant on harrow *peak*
> *Intent to* hear his *harmony* in *sky*
> *And seas that* mumbled *diatribes nearby*,
> *Did grasse*s cogitate and greenly *speak*
> *To* ear *of green, that* blue *and* wave *were bleak*?
> *Did* he *see* clear *and exile gulls scale high*
> *And* unbrinked *cliffs of air in misery*,
> *Venting* inherent tack *with* cornered *shriek*?
> My friend, no *doubt you* sapped a *blue*
> From *sea and froze, in part, some* form from all
> *Quicksilver clues that* titillate the *noon*

Above your crown; but he avers *you flew*
No neurosis *with* the *gulls, nor heard green* call
Of blades *whose* orisons would importune.

First, how do I know the order of the versions? There are four pages of typescript (no real manuscript survives): one draft, with first and second carbon copies; another ribbon draft. As was his usual practice, Blake made pencilled revisions on the first carbon copy, leaving the ribbon and second carbon copies intact. As for the other ribbon draft, it was obviously made from the hand-revised carbon (another of Blake's usual practices). Three versions, then: (1) a typescript and its second copy; (2) a hand-revised first carbon; and (3) a typescript based on the revision. Not all of Blake's manuscripts and typescripts fall so neatly into line, but 'Overtones' offers a typical – and, I hope, explicable – pattern.

Second, why do I choose the first version over the second and third? I am sure it is clear that nearly every change the poet made represents an attempt to complicate or adorn the original wording, to *coagulate* the verse and work it into as thick a mass as possible, a tendency Blake shared with his contemporary, Robert Lowell. Surely the near-monosyllabic ease, the variable idiom and pace of

> *Above your skull: though one is sure you flew*
> *But little way with gulls, nor heard green din*
> *Of grass whose greetings will arrest the moon.*

are closer to the poem's subjects – and to the poet's object – than the thickened, stumbling, Babylonish dialect of

> *Above your crown; but he avers you flew*
> *No neurosis with the gulls, nor heard green call*
> *Of blades whose orisons would importune.*

I think it is no wonder the poet chose to abandon a question beginning, 'Did grasses cogitate and greenly speak / To ear of green': Pope would

29

have welcomed it to *Peri Bathous*. But the original poem is bright and accomplished; and it is the best and most orderly of Blake's juvenilia — that is, of those poems which did not earn a place in his *Prolegomena*. Other early work, strained and eclectic — one piece is actually titled 'The Numidian Bishop As Virtuoso' — I have chosen to omit, along with some fragmentary translations from the German (Hölderlin's *Patmos* and two of the shorter classical poems) and a respectable but stilted 'Soliloquy,' after the *Elektra* of Sophocles.

An extraordinary poem, written about 1945, is called 'Emergency.' Blake took great care with it, especially with the first stanza. Four full versions exist — a manuscript, two typescripts with hand corrections, and a final draft — together with two intermediary attempts at the first stanza. Here are all versions of the opening stanza, in a sort of interlinear construction. (I have italicized the final one.)

1	And first off there was nothing but what was	a, b, & c
	Only biases in being, germs, but this	d
	Certain biases in being, germs; but this	e & f
2	Impacted by eternal chairs that stood	a
	Infused by eternal chairs that stood	b
	Inspired by eternal chairs that stood	
	Imprinted	
	Impresaed	c
	Was filled by light, a wet, oak chair that stood	d
	Soon stuffed with glaze, a flesh, oak chair that stood	e & f
3	A solid moment in a solid hour.	a & b
	Eternal moment in a solid hour.	c
	Eternal minute in a frozen hour.	d
	Eternal solid in a frozen hour.	e & f
4	And next the question posed, the remarked pause	a
	And then the question posed, feared antithesis	b^1
	And then the question posed, shunned antithesis	b^2
	And then the question posed, the shunned antithesis	c
	To be was blunt enough, the shunned antithesis	d

To be was brusque enough : the shunned antithesis	e & f
5 That chairs could move and slide and oaken wood	a
That chairs could slide, could move, that oaken wood	b & c
That chair could slide, that oaken rectitude	d, e, & f
6 Could crack and break and shed the oaken power	a
Could crack and break and shed the oaken stasis.	b
Could crack and break and peel an oaken stasis.	c
Could crack and peel ———————— power.	d
Could peel and crack, pointed insolent power.	e
Could reel and crack, pointed insolent power.	f

This is the artist at work, penetrating to the roots of an idea – not, as in the third version of 'Overtones,' mulching or overfertilizing words. All the changes work to advantage: the dropping of 'eternal' from line 2 to 3; the shift from 'chairs' to 'chair' in line 5, and the 'rectitude'; the introduction and rejection of the weak 'stasis' in line 6, and the adoption, migration, and final transmutation of 'peel.'

In his last years Howard Blake worked on a genealogical poem. He was obsessed with thoughts of his sister – I have mentioned the 'Sestina' to her as Memory – and of his dead 'family.' He sought restitution in a long poem that was to search his origins. The fragments that survive reveal new experiments in cadence and meter, but even the more or less complete sections are radically unfinished. I have not included any. It is worth noting that Blake's work on the poem antedates Lowell's *Life Studies*, and that, like Lowell, Blake was changing his style. Having come through the extreme formalities of such poems as 'Emergency' and the 'Sestina' (as Lowell was to, in 'The Mills of the Kavanaughs'), Blake trying to work out another *phrase*.

A reader coming to Howard Blake's poems for the first time may find himself both attracted and repelled – my own first impression – and, should he wish or need to persist, may have to 'give' more than he nowadays expects to. For Blake's verse, wrought as it is, yields unwillingly, and its effect has a great deal to do with the effort taken to read it: it seeks mastery. Two stanzas struck me upon reading through the poems;

I find myself returning to them as markers, or signals, of what the poet could do at his best – and of what he had to say, with variable imagery, time and again. They are the opening and closing stanzas of 'He Thought to Utter Ocean,' Blake's last finished work.

> *The word is suitable for oceans,*
> *The human dipper, hollowed ledge, man glass*
> *Where water may be captive and of use,*
> *Contained, articulated so presentable.*
>
> .   .   .   .   .
>
> *Sea is the pain whose birthplace is within*
> *The front incisor and whose haze disclosures*
> *Cannot end until each several cell is won,*
> *Each fixed assumption is transmuted to*
> *The agony of dead thing in the bone.*

That the word might be suitable for the final transmutation of the flesh is the 'thought' of 'utter ocean.' In the sea Blake finds that amniotic source the painful truth of which 'Cannot end until each several cell is won.' The pun on 'won' is inevitable, and typically Blakean; indeed the authority of these lines – their sure absorption of 'The human dipper, hollowed ledge, man glass,' 'Each fixed assumption' – is characteristic of the man and the poet throughout. The 'pain ... whose haze disclosures / Cannot end' is the same 'fire / That singes haze with no solution' in the poem on turning twenty-three. But the sea once 'undistinguished' (1937) is now 'within' – 'captive and of use' (c. 1955): in all his last poems, 'sea' is the final and only pain, Blake's raging constant. '*Utter ocean*,' perhaps another pun, is all but impossible – a mixture of memory and desire, of time present and time past ('Contained, articulated so presentable') in time future. For Blake, 'Because the water has receded from the skin / Poems are' (1945). And, 'Perhaps impossibles, when known, are rest' (1950).

32

The Island Self

OVERTONES

While you were standing close to needled peak
Intent to wring far harmony from sky
And sea that dirged its diatribes nearby,
Did grass peal subtle murmurings and speak
To you of green – that sky and sea were bleak?
Did you see stern and exile gulls scale high
And topless cliffs of air in misery,
Venting indigenous pain with shattered shriek?
Bold Herakleitos, doubtless you drank blue
Of sea and froze, in part, some beauty in
Quicksilver clues that titivate blue noon
Above your skull: though one is sure you flew
But little way with gulls, nor heard green din
Of grass whose greetings will arrest the moon.

From 'Prolegomena to Any Future Poetry'
(1936)

ANALYSE DES AMANTS

Yes, I would weep, but tears are not enough.
Nor would a wind-blown, cool, redundant laugh
Articulate the counterpoint I hear
Cavorting like wan twilights, or a clear
Ice dawn on lucid countrysides ... Blush of
Confusion, then a shrouded gazing far
To nothing, breathes the four-four beat in love.

Could Pergolesi improvise from words
The monody his fevered thinking heard
Stringing from star to star in brittle notes?
He was, I feel, long silent till her ghost's
Pale eddying etched greyness on the hard
Stones of her hall. Her death roused sleeping throats
That sang his love like prisoned silver birds.

REBELLION

With acid undulate unrest,
The ageless escalade of mind
To an ultimate wear has blessed
With gaunt quiescence, I defined
The passkey to this sibylled pool
Of peace, and hoped my mind to lose
The purple need, to render cool
And clear this warmth the flesh would choose.

Destroy desire and need desire
For states beyond its flame of mist:
Flesh thirst foredooms me to the fire
Of passion-riddled thinking, twists
Those contrapuntal thighs where brain
Would concentrate on stars again.

MR ALL DITHERS

I

If he could care to hope for cabbages
Their rotund jade might jostle him to peace.
Is scaling shining summits, he cannot
Desire when scaled, the footless destiny
Of imaging Toledos on the wind?
If synergy were all there could be no
Green shoots that symbol super melody;
And he could fornicate with emptiness
Cavorting vacuums in a barren room
Of brain.
            But phoenix is a sign of dreams
With discontent to rest as dreamless ash:
And goals are shallows he would find and keep
Until their soothness breeds satiety ...
Hope that unrest will wash the teetering soul
With paler though a purer purposing.

II

Immaculate redundancies of stars
Corral nomadic strands of Bethlehem
And quiet of the tolling sepulchre.
And if the Wyrd pricked bud which bled within
That satiate time of Caesar's afternoon
Would seep its incandescence through dry pores,
Persuading him of veinous potency,
Then he might point the point in urgent circles.
But hope for guidance by stigmated shine
Is poroused with haze-penetrative doubts.
Future, with flakes of flame he knows as love,

May conflagrate in fusing labials
The harbor of an absolute, of peace;
For love is known to nail minds to that light
Burning the bricks and waves in sight of Him.

RORATE COELI DESUPER

All GLORIA IN EXCELSIS *cry,*
Heaven, erd, sea, man, bird, and beast,
He that is crownit abune the sky
Pro nobis Puer natus est.
             – William Dunbar

See shivering star joy-undulate
Where seeded peace is sent.
With stark reared stone at starving bone
Flesh mitigates content,
And vultures kiss fed flame that is
Voracious to invent.

Salvage tombed wings, three-personed God,
That deep and dazzling dark
May batter sight with stricken light
And incarnate Christ-spark
Heart-canticles can canopy
With Peter's praying arc.

All fish in flood and fowl of flight
Forsake scents – man, loin feast –
For logos child is virgin son
And birth attendant beast
Lows *Aves* before singing rock,
Lows rune for blood released.

Two Trinity at Virgin breast –
Did adumbrations flow
From it of Christ-side-piercing-spear, spare rood
Resounding pathos, so

Young shepherds' love would vaguely move
With wonder and vague woe?

Day of laugh with shadowed moaning
When black light stooped to skin
And tears ... O Jesus, burning Mary
Saint-breast, built you nails then?
Dew church bells beyond chanting stars
Chime birth and thorns for sin.

Concupiscence and cant, these are
God's aptest cradle coil,
Who comes when cups are brimmed with lusts
And lingers until toil,
Sun, love have buttressed flesh not brass
With music for man's moil.

LYRIC: ON OTHER TERMS

These are the quiet leaves wind frustrated,
Zenocrate, within the burnished pulse
And fluxing heart. Silence. These are the dead
With rustless grasp no saccharine repulse,
Nor girder grinding westward to stuck sun
Can forge to fear with tempered Rubicon.

For these are fled to fog Hesperides
Where tom-toms boom no more from typing hands,
Where waves of cloister winnow. Wonder these
That never crack at rook's fall reprimands,
Nor know the split of ditches gleaming out
Where one should wade but shores, irresolute.

GOLD BENEATH THE FLOOR

Voice: ' ... *itstimeya ernt alivin. Sell*
    nekties, beabusboy, workinaoffis ... '
Counterpoint: The Jew of Malta

The iron belly of tomorrow grinds
Quick vagrancies of yesterday and now;
And nothing, no nothing can consume
Famished necessity for Abigail
To think upon the jewels and the gold
(The board is marked that covers it ... I'll be
Urgent at the door early tomorrow);
Can consume marmorean hours that munch
Voluting bubbles with a princox air.

Reality is, in the offing, real.
These purple tortoises that dive and float
In rivers of too rapt translucent thought;
These worming backdrops of pellucid navels
And bowels and warm legs that croon the flesh
Accentuate hollows, deaf, nor seeking ears.
Consider Coriolanus, now, and clown
That silo cornucopia of pride:
The pregnant fruits, with jocund, rush-hour grins,
Gesticulate the stars you would not catch ...
But, if the dutiful Abigail would lean
From some chameleon casement (Te Deum
Laudamus), if bubbles will digest,
If, if Proteus were now ...
        Exsiccative blues.

46

Taxicabs clicking impossible *Trivias*,
While Johnnies drool on fireescapes giving the lie
To Romulus. Come, Barabas, your end
Bakes in the brain to a most elegant glaze.

THIS CHANGE IS SOUGHT

Are these excretions from too crowded mind?
These sweatings of Saint Catherine's rubbed bones
Are not defined.

Thumbed Homer gurgle of licentious telephones
Corroborates lethargic paths that bleat
Of inner peace and stillness padding lungs.
Consider, now, pale buds parade in parks;
Moist scarlet fades my monasteried aches,
While in your eyes are twenty thousand sparks
Where prayers, as in their causes, burn to rest.

These deictic syllables are deductive tombs.

This knife of nothing gouged in nothing, which
Brain molds of fumes, kisses unsleeping beads
That scream, unused, through dark unsleeping rooms
Where poppies of oblivion intimate
Decomposition.

                Your soul was made that
You might uncreate
My blood.

                So invoice files belie
Real setting of that lamb's white footstep here.
Is it because threads broke at your sharp eye?

Is it because dime movie atmosphere
Called Oedipus to ripped eyes and to sight?

Because rotten cellars vibrate fetids where
Numidian incense chants need recondite.

Hair licked by cobwebs of your frozen code –
Code frozen because curls must carve it so –
Hair grinning while the soap is glibly sold
To erin maids from brownstone.

                                        South fog rot
This death of princes very heaven blazes!

Am hungry for deed to Dr Arbuthnot ...
Are cocktail cerebrations holy light?
Is this but standing room in crowded halls?

VIVIMUS QUOD VIVIMUS

Sign: PSYCHIC CARD READER (convolves).
In short, she is confused
With a white land, land of ice and right
Which keyholes in the night sky verify.
Where is the Matthew Prior whose spun pen
Drew Alexander's salon to his pink tips?
And all because in trivia was urge
To mark a snow that somehow will not melt
With tram alacrity.
                                    O bronze, to glitter
Before these slits that have no hands to catch;
Or, if once caught, egregiously outshines
That Bacon who, in nescience, blew the world
To hell, and fussed intently through a little time
To do what I must do ... must do in feeling
The stayless transmutation of your worth.
This bronze, I say, (or is the haze within
Translatable into one single word?)
Is always without form, a form so curved
As to break my china trinkets on some earth
And leave no thread between an oak tree's leaves
And roots that rut the reason to a death.
For it is death to live when unend waves
Slip with too bawdy laps over smooth sands
And brown-grey rocks are lost to open lids ...
All this I wept not, I who wept for Dido
Slain. Dido, another bronze at clearance sale,
And paving, pants, and paint but roads to pain,
And pain, romantic moonlight on split marble
Glowing with sea-mist over some distant sea.
Nothing has molded nicely. Bronze never will.
Nothing will do.

ARGENT SOLIPSISM

Now is a bursting in me. Now a fugue
Sprouts in that heart where othertime you broke
Each outbound note of callower crescendo.
For the sky is in this skull and flings
Blue paradigms beyond this breathing's ken,
To be an equanimity like stone,
So quiet as the ether between stars,
Needing no thing nor hoping, where to hope
Must breed a pain that seeps through every vein.

These pontiff syllables may mean to you
No more than pretty sounds of winds that slide
With pointless whimpers through garrets glazed with dust.
But these are words affirming spring and green
Shoots in an earth no other self will sense.
I formulate for wind and ornament ...
You are intent on damask or noon curls
With which birth donored you, withholding wisps
Of thought that ivy and unite disparate brains.

Never to hope. Never to need your trees.
Never to tread the cobbles under lamps
Shedding their perpendicular inane,
Clinging to nothing which is surely grey
Substance floating in bone beneath your waves ...
Needing no self beyond a self I know.

NIGHT STAND

After sweat (lidtaut) clutch and jaculation
when face and phallus drop significance;
after the nescience ebbs, and all elation
flows with a casement wind that moves askance,
why does your sack of skin and flesh and marrow
merge into alleys' mendicant details?

Wherefore exacerbates the mewing now
when seconds seemed but evanescent nails
forging a foss about intacter selves?

(*Cur?*
     non tam latera ecfututa pandas,
nei tu quid facias ineptiarum.)

An hour ago soured Helen to an hag,
and now she is uniterated ifs
where skin has lost sheets' ludicrous barrage.

SIN SANCTITY SOCIETY & SO ON

in the beginning was some word ...

Wield you the trenchant pen. Wield you that knife
Which severs silence brooding on desire.
Pride is the stay that corsets our desires;
Pride concentrates the hips on single love.
Go to, my lovely rose, tell her that shines
So distant and so tinkling on cold wind,
That you will muse on absolutes confined
Beneath your hat, that conscious concubines
Have touched a sensate grandeur in firm loins
And keep their youth as long and with more use.

... All this for Hecuba, while I, gnawing old bones,
Have no delight to pass away stray time
Unless to spy my shadow in the sun
And descant on my own deformity:
And therefore, since I cannot have this lover,
I'll fallow in fume sunlight, thrusting fins
Of pretense, while lone core ferments abuse.

Yes, yes, go far from me,
Never taste a truth beyond
All imagery of this grained mind.
To lose a phallus in a glitter rime,
To quench lust's hollow belly in a dun
Cloud of reasons pro and con,
This is the world, O Calyphas.
This is the world:
                    To dine with well-bred gestures,
Fondling a fork with trademark of the school;
To spend a decent set of hours that one

May improvise some half-tones on some rule;
Sleep with a body old to questing nails,
Talk of the questions no one can resolve,
Bite on an answer dangling from nowhere,
Smile with satiety when some ancient air
(Of Cimarosa, prithee) exhales *Liebestod* –
And you, no Celia, maybe, swarm before bold lids
That twitch and touch your sure oblivion.
Pride for the nonce. Pride girds the groins
With seemly (no, not too flagrant) caryatids.

MEDITATION IN WINTER

Walk pebbled way, some phoenix house,
Some flames to melt daystone.
Chrysoprase? ... yes, yes, it is confest, it is manifest
Will, so well as any tag, mausoleate search.
For now no self-remembering soul sweetly recovers
Its kindred with the stars; no, nor basely hovers
In opiate sentience.
     Joe Praz, butcher,
Smells blood and bloody buttoxes eight hours
And eight hours and eight hours, *ad mortem.*
Hallowed be Joe Praz.
If one could come, not coincide, at her
Then to descend besieged, quite ivory, towers
And mold clay, and make hay from problem
Would giant character.
I say, Diogenes, in sifting truth
Did life, in lilting pregnancy, leer at
You round the shoulder of that acrobat
Who flings her, pins her to an alien sky?
Stars have an Acropolitan divinity:
Stars are so high.
Life, with Mrs Honour in an offing,
Might have its swing.

The function of the rhymester is to sing.
The rhymester must not think.
So vain deluding joys
That fungus in the nighthood of the mind;
So to the sessions of the silent thought
This intellection, hatched of pulse and flesh,
Is consecrate to burning out each sore
That grinds its mist-mouth through the doubting mesh,

Stirs every hair perception –
From Joe Praz
To loam that bares brown body for the sun
To kiss and quicken with novitiate pain.

A meaning, it is meaning I have sought.
Tracing ice dells of sub-sod prism seers
Who trod the cool of olive academes
To pistons pricking blue air with their clang-rents
And breaking God and silence into bits.
These be the sapient atmospheres,
When bellies, cerebellums drop drop tears
For silence.

Three Panels

1935-37

OF ONE IN A DARK, DARK PLACE

These tears, these tears for God, the world, for me.
Perhaps I never plunge beyond the self.
Ambiguous is but a face put on
By one anomalous and desperate.
This manhood, it is not of flesh and bone:
This muscle, it is not the measure of
Their innate song relating every note.
Come, cry with me – bombast and turpitude
Are essenced in a hole where antiphone
Dissenting prelates droning of some rood,
Some iron casket I, unworthy, hate.
(These swelling tags come much too easily
To plead a plumbing of essential self.)
What is the world that one should pull down that
Which is integral I?
The world is wrong? an iron clock that ticks
Upon macadam wastes where iron tracks
Observe and shun the blazoned click of time;
Or, this which I call me,
Which interrupts inditing timeless rhyme,
Is crooked, where the communal straight lines
Diverge, impinge, but have no need to cry.
This is I.
Take up some cross: this concupiscent self
Is without gold or cure.
Die and a wave of silence sweeps you by
The straight lines never billowing nor suffused
With mergency, with pain, with a remorse.

DECISION WERE PANACEA

We, the deflated ones, know that no clutch
Of unleafed branches will enclose the clouds
We need, not knowing:
                                    for in clouds, some say,
There broods a laughter and that untimed crumbling,
All, to the incoherent fog within our trunks.

Wherefore this declamation? What are these birds
Which quite outwing concatenating wants?
Which way this ululation picking at our veins?
This chain cries down the freedom we have dreamed
And turns us numb with our too quick decrease.
   These substitutions tacking down our time
   (Sir, you say their heads are fourteen carat ... well?),
   Grand rapids bureaus when some sense was set
   On studded chests from Ophir, habitant
   In purplestudded passages the mind rejects.

In short, it is to dream that we are set
For only dreaming catches us in snares.
Now listen nicely: the dream is that pink fetus
Which someday will slip out pervasive pain.
To be a robot clicking over roads,
Aloof, with the efficiency of gears,
To be unfrayed by twang neurotic years
Which jitter through the matter, which evoke
The pointless dark of one whose mind was crunched
To tread these corridors we trod for years ...

O lente, lente currite, noctis equi!
The stars still move, time runs, the clock will strike
And these,

        the concentrations of our slick peripheries,
Will close upon us,

           still without the point.

RUMINATIONS AT RAIN TIME

Depressed tautologies of ebb and flow
And general sea which churns the general self.
These flitting skyscrapes, snapshots whose undertow
Adheres, a flitting sentience crooning tale
Of 'Somehow this could never moor at all.'

Now marble and a gilded monument
Were indication this ephemeral
Wraith exiled the abject knee, inhaled the scent
Of hyacinth lowering heaven with its weight.

Transmute me. Wholly work a clock to wake
Deserter who, despite importunate
Turbines that moan of brawn and sweat and blood,
Would veer, would fondle quiet, would await
Some wind to ruffle stone on his behalf.

'*They have all gone into the world of light*
And I alone sit lingering here'
Watching the highhat clouds deck slate beyond this head;
Watching drops smack and shimmercircle pond;
Watching the me, cognitive something dead,
Something, if quick, would twin, would correspond
To outside animates, is wedged (this might-have been
Segment which powders into time the hours aside, alone ...
No job ... starved ... am seventeen ...)
Within grey jell division of this bone.

They have all gone into a square where men
Crack the new cheek and turn and crack again.

BOY AND THE HUMANIST

One who coops young green blowing in his skull,
The haddock-probed insistence of green waves;
One who makes Nero stalwartly annul
The verbs of violets for potent staves,

He will well know how mountains shove between
Him and anemic chair under a shrivelled sun,
Too definite, too wicker, too baldly seen
And destitute of muscled Myrmidons

Who grant to greenness somewhat greenness thinks.
Proclaim division, seek the wicker, learn
That wicker pawns the pain within the sphinx,
That always stars will wink, pull you with cold churn

Of glare and muscle laughter ... learn that curls
And suntanned symmetry (North Cliffs) converge
To taunt ... then learn to sleep, while iron Earls
Chart the approach to stars' consummate splurge.

PARLOR LAUGHTER

What does he do when echoes chime the spine
And festoon viscid grey where he must urge
Echoes to ring in syllables that break
Along some beach where only sandpipers trot?
Maybe this laugh will topple reigning holes,
Will tickle silence inane and intact;
Maybe some coruscation (tho with dwarf
Promise of sunblast) will lurch out and shimmer
In beams which viscid central only half concedes
Could be flame air pointing far valid flame.
Maybe the laugh does refuge, will dilute
Excoriations of, say, moot jumping bean
And of gongs which ooze their plangent oil within
The humid nights sheened with narcotic nickel.
Laugh. Laugh and deputize the laugh
To echo another air, cut wholly from
That ether blossoming between those bones
That might refute your echo's equity.

And yet this hollow knows an iron wind
And grackle which, somehow, will devise
A tongue to trip a center, arcane collusion
Of bird and wind ... rather redundant crash.

What does this always circumambient decree
Mean by this rush to Samarkand
Or to New England hills that hunch,
That mew within their night?
Laughter can etch no epic, only of lamps
Doddering behind dead panes,

Of grails too greenly sought
When grails house habits like
No solid citizen.

WET AT THE HUB

This emigrate London. This jaded growth
Where rain and parboiled sky must gird us in.
Rain is a want to lushness, nothing loth
To inculcate starched rectitude in sin.

Go, where the aristocratic flamingoes
Unctuously pussyfoot the luke of marges,
And you may stalk the color where shell toes
Sponge nutriment from wet. Nothing less

Oppressive breeds brothers for Priapus
Than sitting compassed by all wet and Cromwell:
To bow a comely head in sooth, would rape us:
We note that dust or brawn monsoon is Hell.

So, in the manner of New England makers,
We moralize the matter; we connote
Design with sky, deep purpose where slob slurs
Of Mrs Mulligan spells antidote

To Right in other undulates than this:
Here fishback unobservance of a tale
That can accrue, with tweedledee antithesis,
To wet deems china adequate for stallion male.

THE YOUNGER COMMUNIST POETS

on Reading S S

These, the boys with corded thighs,
    Who sing us songs of red and fallow brown
    That somewhere will zoom down
    An unsold west.

'Let us chant, in phallic chorus,
    Of warm seed in groins not secret,
    And the girders pinching eyes and
    Memories will go by, will be let
    To kinesthesias brawned to reprimand
    A crackling skin, the palpitating hand.'

These boys with blonded hair
    And lips, firm meteors of blood,
    They are not castrate.

'All festered marrows leave is brotherhood,
    Seize this, we who have understood
    The old worms beneath the white rocks.'

ON HIS BEING ARRIVED AT THE
AGE OF TWENTY-THREE

This much to be, when light convenes to hear
The mellow hide taut over fuming heart;
This is to be a man, broached by desire
For man who glints, an equipoise, in stark sun,
Glints with his meaning shelled within his sphere,
Thinking haze consummations, counterparts
To your Ben Nevis.
                  Break out the fire
That singes haze with no solution,
Break out that need for eyes to smile, to lend,
In certain quiet, beacons that blaze peace:
This were enough, if years must ooze to years,
This were the final stone to weight one here.

To be another year, another ell
On aimless architecture, impertinent
To brain and shorn of all the still heart's point;
Willing to sing, enamored quite to please,
Tonight immense, some hours to distil
In murmurs toward an undistinguished sea,
Leaving the boy's specific continent,
Bleached by the enervation of idea.

THIS CATHOLIC, COURT THIS,
THIS MYRIAD MIND

O be, be more than shopworn microcosmos.
To flare, in pictures that will whip the brain,
Horizons wending beyond appetite.
Half in each phrase steams from halfburied lust:
To realize, through bricking pink and white
Cottages and sprouting them where alien leaves
Rustle silk patches on air, what remains;
To identify with bronze men who must fight
Their fight against your selfconstructed self.

This alley with valiant, its strangled trees,
Demands and goads your transmigrated sense.
O flare, O flare and brick new commonwealth,
Blister the very heavens with your eyes.

Leave the you alone ... alone you are ...
Alone. These coatracks are so erudite
In steel and botany and lavatories:
They, and this cowering self, find recompense
In blunt breaths?

                    ... For you a swirl more solar.

Tear down the rampart flesh, court but a ray
Of foreign light to wreck it and dismay.

1937, EUROPE

PERHAPS FRAIL MEANS

Determined by the indeterminate
He sidled, loth to hoist his moist commitments,
Across the Liffey and beyond what state
Where luke wisteria paints antic cement.
He felt it in his blood. Surely he knew
That Oxford, London, Paris or Algiers
Coffined the potent nail, the privy rue
Patent to cancel disyllabic slurs.
Or were they slurs, these prick triforiums
Always beyond my own mind's habitat,
Always persuasive of adjacent slums
Where answers jangle in far sharp or flat
But not the key, but root of incept nave
Focussed to breathe triforium and choir
And shadows stencilled but too thinly seen.
So, eye, go up: this up must surely have
A nearer eye. Always to gulp that fire
Which slakes no parch nor knows why it has been.

GRINZING: OESTERREICH

To wallow over waves slitting at time,
Lost to brain rock which can mean no blooming thing
Other than silence and decisive rims:
To wander with too certain hope, attuned
To certain music stroked to wring
Attainment of the granite antidote
Which flutters, somewhere, far
To fire or night or other fluid air,
This is the blonde hair song, the too fat peach.
Never to break, to rot, to plain along
Intent on rotund now where this rotund
Conspires to rot. Always to feel sky heart
Urgent between the mucous some time more.

IS THERE NO PLACE WHERE SUN
WILL GILD THE FLESH

Is there no place where sun will gild the flesh
With polonaise not paling towards dark lento,
A place where a steady generous eye
Will light and skid to generous indigo
Swirling around these facets which are I.
I have awaited dawn amongst mosaiced crowds
Who seek a sun peculiar in donation
Of spans between cores waiting for egress,
Each anxious palm too certain that the one
Who would be mirror yet perfecting dress
Could not be that slate face across the square.
I, too, have loitered with them, could believe
The light had built a grove around the core
Instead of golden doorways to receive
Jammed apprehensions searching for the door.

ACTION OF MUSIC

Only to stay this formidable mood for always, –
And contravene the bluing thunder which is wont to intervene
Me and the summit apposite of curls, curls that would say
Tonight there can be silence and a joy but never tune
Of *l'indiscrete*, that tonight may build a yellow stone
Facade which will endure against chill rapes of nights
That do not know the twist and turn of notes that feed the side
With sustenance in mountain magnitude.
You can be calm now, no frost gale can blow
Between the exposed rib, for now the isinglass
Of soft cantata wholly warms and will speak
The cairn of an enveloped still.
The curl that seemed the certainty of sky and sod
And vein has been usurped by concentration
On a dolor, and the peak of dolor
Dresses dark to come in golds and reds
And tunes the dark articulates in threads
Trained to redress that old expectancy
Young rib has fleshed since rib had girdled hope.

IS THERE A WORD TO BURST
THE SUBTLE SKIN

Is there a word to burst the subtle skin
Fixed by that random fist which braves no rain
Of lone belief that lone will terminate
In that one last assault? What is violin
Which spurs demarcate skull with anxious strain
Of possible red apples? Is it that
The syllables gain sense from ambient
Incisions placed with the scalpel under
Your expectant balls? Is sense the final
Hedge which clamps us one? Or is the bent
Sound and long pulse and carving hunger,
Bruited across the sheer swells where a fall
Of no strange falcon is, but that mirage
That yet will point and yield to no now age.

ANOTHER BLUE BLOOM

And there you were. Somehow, (I cannot vouch)
Immediate you was moated, full beyond
The net of me which would but would not catch.
Why, why this need, why do whispers scratch the heart
With need of you, cork insulated sound.
Surely there is, on an aloof plateau
Where minstrels splash the ear with final bars,
The note that plucks this need from captive blue
That blue may join some sea where blades of smoke
Wrest anonymity, the still reward.
Here is a granite virgin, hands shred by ignorance,
Attending rape from leaves in unguent air
Or from that red youth forever hallooing,
There, where boy hair with cur stirs in a breeze
Let from the oaken casement.
                                      This were a sign
For concentration on a single stair,
For detour of those steep ascensions which
Drain off the blood and splotch its red upon
Distant repletion of that too red star.
Things hint the facet brain which broaches hopes
Too catholic to house one finite laugh.

TIDAL PATTERN

To look at you and stew in decreed fumes
Of difference. Always the smoke I clutch
Construes an alien you, one tall beyond
The brush of palms pledging transcended rooms.
Where is the prod of blood which will outwatch
And smother silence managing this fond
Abeyance. Why does a smile, automatic crack
Of a glass plain, slide bowelward and break
Its pregnant news where no news can be read.
(Deliver this too cogitating stack.)
Either arch roofs across expectant ache,
Tops to taut cells whose tolerance is bled,
Either redeem blind lighthouse from the night
And donate rays and wrecks for company,
Or beam the bowels with adamantine oak
To bulwark them from polyphonic bite.

So sure of singularity, the we
Reject new roof which, through being, must evoke
New need, haze hope, anesthetic of stone lips,
The hewn preposterous of fingertips.

SLIGHT RECKONING

Here we may brood awhile. Here let us sit
Unwinding what it is to love and hate,
To feel the want which clangs along grey halls
Peeled of faith that soon blood rug and apposite
Gold cloth could clothe. Here let us gulp where late
We thought to sniff with certainty of full.
Now let us sit and build a plan for now
That will erode the holes which fester us.
Now let us point to that one voice unheard,
To that bright curl just broached before the prow
Of cafés split possible release. To alter us
Let us draft maps which will chart pain a word,
For syllables are ointment to spent brains
And sounds will gild grey corridors bereft
Of more conclusive ore. Root to a stand
Where lonely snow can yield its full remains,
Where drifts can pluck a laugh from their cool toft
Which points the worm in plains of idiot white sand.

THEN EYE WERE CLEAR

You cannot come again. Words I have shed,
Pedestals which bruit identity, are
Not ambiguous and their unique glare,
While it scales toward the rivetting of me
In granite space heretofore inane,
Toward required dawn in too egregious dark,
Splinters the tensile filament you forged
Till barren filings splash on foreign ground.

Yet had you stroked and tasted codes of me
You had been, now perhaps, that nebula
I divinized would catch a castle here –
Perdurable flesh of incandescent trees
Which, sometimes, evince green breaking the breath,
Which chats, too timorously, 'Now it is
The bark in liberated sight.'
                              But now,
Blue petal is a brimstone cheek, perhaps,
The cobblestones which bleat urbane despair.

THE EXPECTATION

Is there an eye outside the mullioned pane,
Face to convert the eddies which toll here
Where no thing disports cacophony?
Yesterday knew no answer, and today
Portends tomorrow quite significant.
And yet to know would be to concentrate
Tensile and potent fingers on this pulse
And now would shatter always in a clutch
Of 'Here I am, this need needs remedy.'
Yet here is hunger coils its barred refrains,
Slides while it surges in its mist suffusion,
Eager redemption castrate in a mist,
Scalpel of steam the brain aspires to blunt.

1938-1942

EXERCISE: TO A MODERN
PHILOSOPHER

In this non sequitur there is a ring
Will rout the wires you weave to win 'the cup.'
And every blade congener of my fling
Will castrate logic with a muscle fillip.
Surely you knew your sounds could show no flesh,
That hasty dives slitting towards certainty
Would hatch a dormouse doubt, soon would enmesh
You in dumb unity, would, happily,
Burst bravest strings of steel and toss you, bare
But urgent, to sow nicer subtle blades,
Uncertain whether snow teeth biting air
Or certain sirloin words soon would invade
That satin puff you perorate to reap
Summer until your chill brain's final sleep.

STILL, TILL RIGOR BREAK

Till golden twitterings grind pain and sight
To notes upon the bars of time's fine music,
And earnests of tall doors (with pastorals,
Redemptive of this waiting with small breath,
Flooding across the waiting eye, beyond
The sill that bottoms doorways, and must do)
Come to deliver or to demand the body,
I shall not move to meet tongue trumpettings
That lend macadam point and wreathe for men
Illusion of nice solder between palms.
I must be still and hope no catapult
Drawn to confound those distances I feel
(Feel has speck sound, real zero on this tree).
Give me that parcel of belief you own,
Or seem to, that calls air your path
And paste and solders you to those
Who seem to murmur around too curbed corners,
Who fly to suns on my unsure approach:
These bones will move though sub-skull grey hills say
That moves are billows breaking on that sand
Which never can be water or a wave.

I HAD NOT KNOWN THAT
YOU COULD BE SO TALL

I had not known that you could be so tall,
That I had charged anemic vessel to peer up
Too far, and, now, the height may claim its own
(At least, an own to eye), breaking the call
Of vessel to its fundamental stirrup.
There was deep thread might strand me to that lone
Integer I have long groped in nighthood for,
But, now, the cliff you are, the sterling rock
Has splintered those foundation notes and cast
Plausible magnet dowering this visitor
Mite license to pursue its paradox
Of two steel cellars though the first be last.

TRANSCORPOREAL WANTED

There is little, somehow, one can say
Abrupter than the green thing, the now thrust,
The brute push of starved fingers to reach God
Within the framed avoidance of your corpse.

These words may tell you nothing, but must say
That in one gravel night within a room
Blood braced to speak.
                          These words are stars that are
In quiet and in token of a sense,
Token of that flame which can distil
All void, all torment, and redeem
Imaginings of what a still star spells.

But words have bruised the tongue, the tools of thought
Rasp on the rusty tongue, corrode the cool
Of said, and tell no silence till the night
Shivers with flares of what this silence speaks.
Here let the word give birth and boom a brain
Across, within, confronting that recess
Where veins compute the sum of what should be.
Let pulse waves crush egregious shells that cut
The me from you, each hair thing from the rest,
For shells deform our meet magnificence.

CONSCIOUS IMMERSION

Now core and core will touch for the sun-blacked second
(Every man-molecule set for the signal that walls
  Can evaporate, lines become line,
  Centers can whip to a whole which no hand
  Ever could extricate, ever reform)
  But frost from space where star accepts discretion
(And sports identity but pawns completion)
  Lurks to pummel the ear, to pestle us
  To several chips the anxious blood had felt
  Might crown the core in sold-short certainty.
    There was song, strophe chafes the skin: speech
    Must out to smother prolix eddies which intone
    That speech can rinse no aggregated coals;
    Nor can we sit and stare on static mountains,
    For peaks will pierce to planet places
    And exhaustion steams and numbs
    That peaks should pull the eye too high for note.

The tempered grace and grail is anchor that would be
Unquestionable hitching-post and plaque
To fell and fullest sight of blood's bass traffic with
Inevitable dangle and the cut
Implicit in the shadow and in line,
Ravel and speck, all other.

There is no rest till we know guarantee
That inner underbrush, after the scythe has lopped,
Is pregnant field, coherent in the sun.
Evidence of a gold, beyond fat ore
Cool womb compiled; some muscular device
That broaches gold adjacent intent eye;
Some worth that worries jungles into groves

Is what the clear core knows must be construed.
Now a positive, blue air must blare its blue
(For first breath, not so often, nets a core
That cannot tarnish nor dilute its April glaze
Which is to speak, always to hunt, not to forget)
An incandescence that will deluge order
Through accustomed gloaming of the practical streets,
For natural night would force a flame to fan itself.

PONTIFICATE THE SELL-OUT

The long approach, up trails of blue and white
And stone and fir and varnishing lichen,
Is blocked; while, in that place,
There breathes the still both of a bite
And of desire that prone space be all in all.

Not long ago cultured belief that stones
Were likely to be bottomed by the beams
Of a stocky star, tactile, yet would be
Thought and corpuscle in resolution.
Today, while eyrie star lags biased in idea,
Blood absconds with drive, thought and need remain
Wedded, blandly insistent of the marrow
Gnawing out its sweet, adamant in saga
Of compact, of genetic consummation
In bloated expectancy and deliberate hope.

But now, in each place, thorough bass drones that
In nows no sense can word, that no cell spreads
Equal to each note that trips the heart
In bruising ideation.
                                    Instant
The ruin that contaminates a sky in the
Too credible crepuscular, becomes
Motley translation of the focal heart
Which cannot ken the fun in being foiled,
Which must not think there is no ore in all the vein
Intones with final throbs about a final beach.

The death, it seems,
Is tragically to utter mountain sound
Without decorum of the boards and plot
The nothing needs to narrate its deep end.

But now, at last, we must learn to skim the milk,
Reduce the philosophic cow unto dumb udder
Or to that just-shared shit cow does allow.

Only dilutest auditors for inward words.
The certain self is justly alien
But would see answer ambushed on that height
Which arterial prophecy has descried
Could spell the space that cramps this night.

LITTLE CAN BE DONE ABOUT IT

Some boyhoods soar (eschew psychology)
Like kites that waltz upon a salient wind,
Never gavotting, O wind banks, never groggy
With inner thickets which, time out of mind,
May ground the slickest kite that is unwound.
Waltz boyhoods implicate jade mistletoe
Over white doors, speak some affectionate
Sun margin: But (and turns were apropos)
Boyhood kites must have a slant, innate,
Implicit, not contrapuntal with the weight
Of sobs outweighing major-laughter eighths.
Today freckles have, in retrospect, a sound
Which flecks bright saucers and our arranged breaths
With draughts of rock till form drops to sharp ground.

THE TRANSLATED SILENCE

for Robert Luce

I

Did you, O Variant, at first, to flatter us
To brim, did you design us winners of
Some paste (as light transpires) topaz that, now, our loss
Might prove ten times as much.
                              Or wherefore Chartres
Which, and unexpectedly, was bricked and hewn
Under a sky which fenced quite other tunes?

Man ... who screeches nails upon ephemera,
The final flower of hair tautologies
Which have, as essence, tentacled inane.
There is glare Helen (no Ilium's Waterloo)
Who scrubs at blueblood marble day on day
(Each finger stamen which might have wed the bee)
 And for a figment, custom-built, this ayre! (the pay
 Is ten good dollars, Miss) pink stamens sea-change
 To dun whitlow (now, Variant) which may
(So sympathy between anomalies) point to
 High concept of concern between those stars
 That bolster each the other, elegant, in line,
 Precise ... so, good.
(Better to prate rat and madman and, sometimes,
 Emerge with suntanned sentence stuffed with sage.)

II

Where, where that first mover? Like cerement frost
Ice silence bruits conceited sirens from

89

This ear to Mars. Silence will vent
Nabisco avatars.
It is we who house the space.
To think is wallowing through allusive woods
And, not to think, were boar grunt-tusking roots.
Silence, with apoplectic, cudding vocables,
Clumps down air stairs and hits upon
Some floating, yet unborn, yet immanent
Mistake.
           And silence is that ghost –
And crucibles protest the ghost absurd –
Which makes now steak, now shady cities where
Those palm trees drip GOD attar into guile
Freed of neurotic mercury of self,
Connote a dangling stillness beyond hands;
Which flagellates each vein, which whips the hair,
Which sows its welts on ripe earth which must hear,
Which contravenes the necessary hope
Till universal echoes spell the brain's fell counterpoint.

CREDO ESSAYED

Cogitant rock must plop, but not until
The bowel lamp can pumice purpose here.
Heart's basic flame must conflagrate, it can
Concede no fort for dark, it must insinuate
Lucid scout-sparks to rinse the insane halls:
It scales to purpose while it storms to sight.
Heart has no need to need cackle bomb that splits
Virgin sidewalks that wend to counties thought:
The blue eye glitters, now, to an indubitable
That guarantees the self, that charts the golden crux,
That queries puzzle of smack entire cottages
When boards themselves body board enigma,
Irrelevant when all corpse must be fixed.

Cities drowned under sky may mean for GOD,
But GOD sums meaning to the fractured faith:
Perhaps only GOD is the intent of hands
Which layer proud bricks to launch a corpuscle
That, minute by minute, can be crumbled
By arrogant arm which deems
Its basic flame the meet incineration
For divers flames that gnaw through night to day.
Let us admit night halls a baby state,
Examine silence lodged behind the lung
And plumb its black till sod confirm the hunt.

These Questions for Balance 1936-(1943)

THESE QUESTIONS FOR BALANCE

for Eleanor Blake Warren

I THE MATTER

Speak, deploy the vein and all the vein
Can spell and all the vein must act because
The brain demands. Speak granite that will still
Sense of wrought peninsula, speak till words
Breathe and foment within their given flesh.

So was said:
                These pilgrims who skin sound kneecaps
Before Cipher, would smother self (each thing breeds tears)
Before white virgin have never known this
Nor can ever know the varimetal eyes
That tinkle Cipher's death.

                        (There is a canyon where
Sunset is full shackled until time
And spatial acrobatics fall asleep
And I would never see it, never need it,
Never witness that torment of sunset trapped
In stone.)
         No Word is ever spoken now,
And Life which gave its life is, now, without
Its Life.

    Bleed this,
O blazing dark, render this face a flower
That never wilts, nor ever can be known,
Nor hoods a meaning which discretive bone
Exiles beyond boy hands that must clutch scent.

II TIMES AND NOW

Perhaps we lost much, lost myopia
Which swaddled dad in clouds.

                                 No sacrament
Of swords, no chitchats trek between taciturn
Far stars (effluvia of Emanuel
The Swede's goodneighbor Heaven), no mohair,
No hot tea where assured vowels float
In sure security that, somehow, words were more
Than trellised bridges fainter than an air
Which wisps its fingers everywhere around
But never can be that thing which it meets.

Their outset brawn, hope, faith.

The longest date is narrow or too wide
For marrow to compute deracinate
Hope.

          So, without hope, we turn and weld the head
To mountains seen as marvels, named, the Caesar:
The bounty of a mountain can be caught
By fingers aching from that exercise
Of snatching odors which will float away.
The mountain, the clear boulder, sun or night …
If night bruit cannons to augment itself
The young snagged hands will shiver to the song,
For sun and mountain married in the mind.

Believer Guillaume Postel (where, where have you been
These so seasoned years) believed green world
Grew clean, that skulls grew holy, year by year,
Unless his God broke love and motors men

Had worked, unless good God
Tagged their good no good to It.

Heart is thirsty for a thousand hemispheres,
Too drowsy or too castrate to discern.
In this bleak season (when the bone is pinned
To ground and stars, before the urgent eye,
Flaunt certitude or far immaculate)
Our throats, through the loam drain which is this hour,
Erupt small sound. We are rinsed into that sewer
Where friends learn men are equal, hills are neither
Cyclops nor Titanias, but are
Cast into that stature which thought carves.
We cry to What, and What can bud no word.
We raise an arm, and What watches us?
We mold in jail, half lost before we were:
And like a rock beneath whose burden lies
The enigmatic worm that atrophies,
We have small will to rouse, we have no brain to rise.
Nor can the stars rejoin to speech where blood
Is frozen by a pain that knows no let.

The dad is dead. The answer that is ours
May be the certainty that answers are
But splinters in space floating on this view.

III THE SUBSTITUTION

Can I propose (although I know no Christ)
That you should pray as Paul and Peter prayed.

Silence shoots here while wind begets white pearl
So precious, without spot, which, without God,

Becomes God.
                    And the thighs and the hot lush
We bruise with steel lips that seek the goal
In damp red, and the blush of the hard nipple
On hard breasts
(The crown is chaste, the bust, a nunnery)
And the devouring, the swarmlocusts of that breath
Which, in bone penthouse where ghosts float, asserts
That love's young dream will find fog incarnate,
These substitutions rear the subsequent inane.

Paul and Peter prayed,
                    not to a trolleycar,
Late and corroding onward down tar space,
But to a What, a flash their minds would mold
In lieu of lips, of our procrastinate peak.

No doubt the nothing stuffed us full at birth
With aptitude for forms to fill our craw,
With need for bricks to build just any wall ...
Clothes on a bakelite gargoyle rife with vacuum.

To set glint muscle stretching for the one
Who may glisten where cicadas drone till night ...
O want ... want ...
                    (Deaf echoes
Break our bland hermaphrodite.)
Where the beloved, the salve to close these boils.
To pray as Paul and Peter. Peter ...

IV THE POLITIC SLANT

We eye the fat men. We have heard
Old magpie chatter when the oriole was cold:
An avatar of cinnabar and halls
Where queen and huntress might stay chaste and fair.
We must hear the jackals breaking cellar panes
For divers fat men fattened on the lithe
Pounds of beef their elders lopped with minimum of blood.

There is cloud, and leaf, and garbage, and top time
Which (crack) confute outsides who understood
Rockbottom is brotherhood.

Nor may the fat men go. Nor may the fat men stay.
Their emeralds, their sofa silence brings
Song through the night: blonde cadences from now
(Which have, in times, poured bottles of the sky
That dust might sprout to mud
And clods might wrench and rise towards blue and light)
Must somehow breathe and spurt
To speak the sterling breath.

Some say: all is changed more than wax under the seal,
That glittering elements compel a novel shine,
That timber pinning rots, that steel must serve,
That sun is withdrawn from the fat flesh
And the high arm must be broken.
We have trudged to the treasuries of snow,
Have primed the silo of our hail,
We have stored love against this year of shellshock,
Against this necessary rape
Of the sequestrated emerald
Locked in the private, columned chamber of the bloated.

If blood were never vapor, if hairs were parallel,
If amity tied fingers to chill tractor,
If flakes of light were fed to every shirt
Then the luminous pulse never need stoop for
The nighttime drumming through grease shirts down there.

We must have light to prove our room is wired
Although no armchairs woo us to that wall
From which the foliate Paul, the rocky Peter call.

V TO WORK, AS MOST MEN WORK

They are not iron who break the hills that feet
May jog towards an implacable mirage
Which will be loam for some, full paraclete
For one who is no nearer iron.
                                    This after age
Which grants no space for dressed kaleidoscope,
Which has mislaid the Mary, which can devise
No passport for Democritus or me ...
Steel, and the force of bulbs' ambiguous juice,
TENDERIZED IS MODERNIZED, GET WHAT
THE BOSS IS READING.
                                    Files must always be
On tap for inundation of white flutter
That augurs quick parthenogenesis of tone.

This Isabel, whose eyes being turned to steel
Would sooner cry a flame than weep a tear;
These ribbons routing intellection's drive
Until day's drummer invocate the surge
Which is sonorous hammers on wet shingle!

And does this silence cry. Sound blood does gush,
Talks, as it falls, and asks them, Why is this?
They, with their nails, would scrape away our blood.
The more they scrape, the more spilled blood blotch is.
Too many dead sounds.
                              O grader, that a lawn
Should never slope, should catch no solitude
From sun and picnics of contingency.

This must go by:
                    tympani skyscrapers
Flatten green words that whisper of the me
And of absurd firs which ply photographers
On the days when Paul and Peter should preach to blasted
    ears.

VI AND, FINALLY

Blank earth is all before us. Neither sleep
Nor answer creeps into the room
Where we have, with such quiet, gone to scratch
Incarcerate mists that will let sun motes in.

Now is the hour of improvising mud.
Our shack is never dry, our hand is out
That Richard may redeem our sepulchre.
The worm is on the skin, the shirt is dust:
And if the skin, the shirt must once assume
(For apathy will blanch a second in defense)
An ancient whole, the worm, the dust will come
Again to sign the second's quixotry.
The days are swifter than hysteric piston,
Are breathed in blunt hope.

We would believe in a Paul's or Peter's Christ
Were wind and skull not crushed with too much air.
The sky is high: long thoughts of a long black
Have circumscribed each eager panacea.
We have no Christ, unless to live alone
Beneath the salient covert of these hairs
Where Caesar and the Anabaptists jostle
Immanent Joe Praz for the rapt hair's ear.
Tomorrow and yesterday ... our brother, you bastard,
Fodder for strong zooms of apt interment.

This retch is seed dropped from delivered spores
Which, too long, have fought to scalp our tented need.
We sketch Himalayas where our fathers seemed content
To arbitrate with thighs and heart and towers.
Give us, O Cipher,
(Though, surely, I know that there is no thing there)
Give us a let from sores, from wings that find
Wings of small use when loam is in no place:
Give us some peace we think our fathers knew.

The questions, the balance, O Harmodius,
(The dark is cocktail to concupiscence
And science that freeze taut fingers with ice glare)
Have made a twilight of insatiate sense,
Have given silence audience, have inscribed
Aloof arkana on chameleon air.

Last Poems 1942-

THE INDETERMINATE IS
HERE AND NOW

The indeterminate is here and now
The vague, the jungle that the will holds back
Is loose and floats itself, its smooching self,
Between the posts that tamed the undertow
Always whirling, in cretin murk, to rear attack,
Withdrawal and a vague abeyance.

Is there no post on which to fix,
No flint concision, certain to strike out
In daylight, this concerting night,
Or only still-born sparks that will construe
The loneliness and loss
Which the vague, the stealing tide
Denotes and points as total recompense
For hope of the terminal and granite light,
For solvent of the fetal appetance.

NOTES FOR AN ELEGY

[*to John Brooks Wheelwright*]

Whether to speak. There are impediments,
You know. It points bleak taste, or none, to use
A friend as peg for ornament to trill
Or starter ribbon that the dexterous pen
Might prove itself again to the few ears
That may remain and listen. Almost two years
And I have waited and weighed, weighed and wondered
And knew in the gut that you would wish good speech
Rather than intent silence; that you would
Want a memorial mound of more than earth,
A mound of words to rear a dolmen where
You worked and lived and worked again to prove
That work could fill the silence that beat at
Your thin electric bones. You sought to prove
The facts that fouled you were quite remediable
In diamond tomorrow. Jammed in the offal of
Blunt now, you needed, and you saw in a beyond,
Fracture in the mud, the pastorale
That little boy with striding March beside
Had needed and had builded for his substance.

As friends, as men we could talk and drink and break,
Or try to break, the shells that separate
Idea from Idea and covered agony:
As poets we could say, 'It is enough
That I think you good and sometime will be better.'

One time you said, 'I see you rather clearly
For, you see, you are so like me when I was
Your age.' I wonder, did you mean that.

Is that the reason why I thought I understood
The rush of talk, the drinks, your thought's sometimes
Exacerbating jumps and towering dives?
Is that the reason why I learned so much
From you as man and manner, but would turn
The head away from your won speech, your poems?
Is that the reason why I marvelled at the way
You'd woven tolerance and tact from knots
That flailed sharp nerves until you found a way?

Something in me will blush that I should speak
Of you in words; something will always say
That speech about you never will arrest
The you, that words are vulgar and may desecrate
The complex Jack that lived in the big house,
Extended it, and was it, and much more.
I speak at all because I hear you say
That speech is all my trade, and all is grist
To trade while shells obtain; that you had rather
Have me construe some accident for you
Than brood in dumbness, too proud to make mistake
In telling of you in a poem or two.
I must speak plainly if I speak at all.
I must not festoon you with tissue trimmings.
I shall tell in prose, if that will do for now,
A prose that sketches somewhat what you were
To me and, perhaps, to a few others.
Sometime I hope to fasten in a thing
The miracle I felt our friendship was:
Now is a mood of notes, of speaking plain.
In short, of *speaking* : not the time for rearing
Indubitable thing which may be you as I
Could feel you.
                    The dolmen you deserve

Will prod me always, but I feel it is a time
To say a word or two to let you know
You prod me to some work and to some words.

I SAW ONCE...

I saw once a grass or flame or seashore rocked
With shells or shored by sand with waves defining
Shore, implying shells, not contradictory
To grass that charged to bull-rush pond
Or flame that crisped the grass once a yellow duration
Had properly infused used green. It was
No simple change to feel the flame derivative
Of flames and a too catholic consumption, or
Impertinent to word eye never stroked
Nor tired acceptance cloaked; it was a crass,
Ignoble retch, when every several vein
Queried sea, shore, shell, sand and queried,
Why is this? Is this the way? Does this impugn
Or pose impossibility of sand consisting
In that corporate cloth around idea?
Must the word not dredge, drain and quite inform
Potential sand and shells to decorate
That terraneous conflagration grown brain knows,
The idiot walls that block
Awful entablature of the immanence.

BECAUSE THE WATER HAS RECEDED
FROM THE SKIN

Because the water has receded from the skin
Poems are. Because beloved has defined
Its self, and outlines, other than the sketch
Within emergent, have resisted and
Remained always the other (as it should be)
Sounds gestate till a perfect plausible,
A thing pruned of its papules is.

One had not meant to speak, one meant to be.
The truth (or selfishness) ruled out the reasonable:
Inherent stuck (coherent) loyalty to me,
Compulsion to parade entirety
In comely, because just, coercing flesh.

Intended speech is private though it jog,
In noble loan, the general selfish ear.
Not compromising because it cannot merge,
The poem burgeons, is an island self.

THAT COUNTERFEIT COMMUNITY
WITH JOE

That counterfeit community with Joe.
And differences do not just dissolve,
They are denied and dive, and through
That comfortable denial
Is born a guilt, anxiety and sweat,
Belief in demons and the singe of Hell.

How can we face the grim addition to the self
Which piling minutes point? How can we keep
A necessary pride and recognize
That now is richer for a recent hemlock seen
In loneliness but with a general balm.

The challenge must be met. Choice is rhetoric:
For pebbles and all other evidence
Will cairn above the ear or grin before the eye;
And nightmare looms in incorruptible defense
Against the myth of general unity.
To include and see, then backroads may debouch
On surer concrete or on antiseptic shores.

EMERGENCY

for Matthew Finn, Jr.

Certain biases in being, germs; but this
Soon stuffed with glaze, a flesh, oak chair that stood
Eternal solid in a frozen hour.
To be was brusque enough: the shunned antithesis
That chair could slide, that oaken rectitude
Could reel and crack, pointed insolent power.

Always the current of the unmoved air
Would wrinkle impulse bent on a retreat
Towards silence and the quartz of primal cave:
Lodged nerve would pound, would sprint to cadence where
It had propounded single tune to beat
In bars to cup a wind and cage the wave.

Certainty seemed to break: that stuttering
Of silence, oak, torn air, the index pause
Contrived to gestate storm from incidents,
And blood won joy when deafness, anything
Gave thunder period, deployed boy laws
As cellar to each movement's accidents.

Insistent others tolled that veinous thought was lone;
That contrarieties of solid oak
Were normative; that the beamed plea, droned in
Each vein for static acre, could not own
To excellence of when the solids broke,
Nor word a rune that would erase the strain.

Now it is war: and heart must bruise young hand
Searching amongst far pine tree on stone hill
For oak that will stand still, be company.
Fraternal hand grips a dismay, demands
Fair payment for this wound, when wind and will
Dissolve to spasms: cheated, no granite key,

No necessary tonic the ripening ear
Had heard, had needed, had scooped up with breath.
Being must fracture fingers to convince
The blood that baby melody was fear
Of thunder, of cleft oak, of those death
Conjunctions that no score can quite evince.

SESTINA TO MEMORY AS
ELEANOR BLAKE WARREN

Your head could never bow to any rage
Beyond your margins. Those blotches on your spire
Became: lichen lives on stone, may desert hope
(Prefigured fog) spume order into hair.
But oceanic fury bleaches bone
Into integrity we call a scar.

One night, within my arms, you said your scar
(O Terminus) would fetch my wanting rage
Long, long before I could infect our bone
With white and terrible whining to a spire,
Smooth the tan topple into the tendered hair, –
The tyrant tower broached as promised hope.

Myelin gave over, gave in to hope,
To wonder, as waves beat trunk to scar
The scorched incredibles of lichen hair
Prone to seclude. Dignity born of rage
Concreted walls until they pitted spire
Beyond support as fenestrated bone.

Forgotten fury worked her fingers to your bone
While they indentured you to give up hope
That your towering locks might burnish your hot spire
As lichen lumines as it turns new scar.
As child, you tossed the knife (child in rage)
Soon to assume your traps of rigid hair.

Too angry (how withdrawn your ordered hair)
To know the flame was ashing each dear bone
That tolled your death unless you talk your rage.
It is not done. Just what had rendered hope,
The tease, the hold-out, manufactured scar
Further to chalk your scarred, corrode your lichened spire.

No bub love and no Tom-boy space, that spire
Would keep its place. Shaking, fingers would mold hair
In place. While, marrow-wise, raw lichen scar
Transliterates the babyhood to bone.
As you staggered neighbors saw (the stumbling hope
You felt to hide) fall dirt-ward to that foremost rage.

Sister, your spire was termited by bone;
The congress of your hair divulged your hope.
Spire reeled and toppled with each scar. We rage.

HABE JA DOCH NICHTS BEGANGEN

Dass ich Menschen sollte scheun;
Welch ein thörichtes Verlangen
Treibt mich in die Wüstenein?

       –Wilhelm Müller

for W. S. Talabach

One hold out he calls hope: it bows the bone
Of innocent today, walls off surprise, and,
With baby mercy, spills immediacy.
For he is armed with warrant that the Right
Nests in the right breast pocket, that the Right
Colludes (outrageous agency) with
The forming hand … (the ineluctable cunning
Of privy designation, – cellar crime
Of the anterior commitment).

                    Blast the left
Rose, turn down the sun, shut off each bulb
That, luminous, might light to awols from
Unspoken though inherent plan.

                     No now could ever be
So here as was a total then that was
Aptest to wipe away the feel of lost boy
Quite alone.

                Who is with eight-year olds
Scuffing the lawn alone on sunlit afternoon
Where possible wrote wonder in the air,
Where actual droned intolerable to the ear
That would have heard a single comrade pin

Had any pin but dropped and pinned the boy
To unity with street and happy dust
And pectoral afternoon, to citizenship spreading
Its anesthesia where pain from being out was felt
Too much to feel.

     This is the burning shadow,
A mislaid distillation that sclerosed
Presenting innocence of importunate,
Infuriating, stubborn, so imperative-to-bend Now.
Still pool of 'Nothing can be done to company
The boy' blanches the million neighbor corpuscles.
Forever in flame because They were not then,
Or, if They were,
Stared Their improbable.

      The pool paupers
Young sun and leaf, is prerequisite idyll,
Adhesive water pattern and impertinence.

    II

To litigate is ... and limn that island day
As continent, accompanied. Not lie but why.
Boy (on time, not tardily) can be this minute
Compound, astonished heir to flow and relevance.
Cerebral arson, out ... rid of the steel (whole-
Annihilating) tracks ... reins slacked, gone purposing
To fire each shuttered house ... here he can brook
Sun deviant from what the drive was.

       And will the boy
Be found? and where? for he abides, perhaps,

With Cambyses or Gulliver or with Akhnaton,
Or wends in coves, whistler of several ayres.
   So silly-wandered late in space that may not toll,
    The boy's accredited, though stray, by moribund Hellos.
Disjunct. To here the boy looks man ... though set
His exile mold, Way too tot to greet
Presenting ore.

         Because the eye is in,
He cannot see how his fulfillment looms.

His antique justice blinds the present innocence.
A Clytemnestra's acolyte, it is his neck bleeds
How bravely as (surely) blade was put
To other skin. But the operable hour
Were never less equivocal.

           He must ken how
To feel a distant dead man before the lids
Will open to his gold molten for incarnation.

10 SEPTEMBER 1950. 4 AM

Baby pitfall: one should be the thing that one admired.
The aim destroys both idol and idolator.
What thing one be and how and why
Is known ... or can be. But that otherwise
Is challenge, is behest. And there is pain
Spawn of the covert outrage:
What is not known must be the excellence one would.
And wisdom, – which is charity,
Is Arjuna who hears, so feels, –
Is distant, welsh, forbidden to a self
Blind to the room peculiarly right,
Deaf to the quiet many things suggest,
Walled from that peace the one sans heroes is –
Oh how can I stand me
As noble mountains challenge and attest.
Perhaps impossibles, when known, are rest.

HE THOUGHT TO UTTER OCEAN

for Peter Risch

The word is suitable for oceans,
The human dipper, hollowed ledge, man glass
Where water may be captive and of use,
Contained, articulated so presentable.

Grateful for continents, an ocean can
Be borne because cerebral eye scans beaches
Beyond billows, recalls the certitudes
Of charted globe, anticipates the order that it must.

Fog on the North Atlantic presses mind
To dis-eased concentration on the ship,
Immaculate steel and hawser, pride in the bowsprit
And screw, a triumph (what time for manners?)
As bow splits water open as the screw propels ...
This fury and defiance is allowed.
The passenger is dry and tidy and amnesic of
The cirrus incoherence beyond rails,
Congratulates himself, his prescience, –
And flat denial that the bulkhead leaks.

Forever minor, child to ocean, sea
May well be fresh enough to quench a thirst,
Though big enough to roil, incorporate,
Should he be careless of his formulae.

The beach is evidence that water can be reft.
Beach is patent no-man's-land, memorial
To outcome of the panic water on
Rock densities whose over-confidence

In diamond certainty, in final shapes
Was ground to minuscules, pounded by drink,
Routed and altered by albino, whitecap molars
Enraged by that still arrogance,
Genetic flaunt of rock boasting
Coherence dry beneath the sun.

Beneath the mathematic mind, his bravest comb,
The water waits.

     Below the luminal artefact
Liquid subtraction.

The lineations he contrives,
The multiplying tongues to tell a tale,
A form, a shape
     (that he may go to sleep
Enough assured because the dark, Damocles air
Is now become familial)
     Behind sonata notes
We string
   (the boldest stare at space, speech to sea)
Is shadow of the boy who whistles lest
Already twilight air solidify
Into black moiré jacket clothing into lung and/or
Bunging the aural cavern with solstitial ebony.

Stars reassure as mind unwinds its threads
And concretizes forms aloof and loyal
In lieu of cobbled sidewalk heading home.
The sea is foiled until its cousin
(Refined ally and somehow self translucent)
Transpires as sympathetic mist
And implicates the mind in night.

The agony of ocean, unwilling guest
Upon the iron bed of happening:
Humoral exigencies of liquidity
Compressed to amputation through stranger Euclid's lines.
Intransigent, it cannot wed the rock,
It must unform taciturn pinnacle
To boulder, pebble, sand, until,
(In arbitration) jointure blooms
In mud.
       Ocean is lonely for it has
No name ... is idiot, choreal, an affront.

Unkin to logic, sea reminds
Its contemplator of his impudence:
Ideographs, his driven imposition
Upon the threat of folly sea is.

Sea is the pain whose birthplace is within
The front incisor and whose haze disclosures
Cannot end until each several cell is won,
Each fixed assumption is transmuted to
The agony of dead thing in the bone.

Preface to the 'Prolegomena'

PREFACE

TO SOME READERS the title of this book will seem egregious egotism. Probably it is. It may mean no more than the restricted obvious: any first book of verse is prolegomena to any other verse conceived, at some future time, by the same writer. On the other hand, it may mean what, in reality, every man, when he publishes a collection of his verse, means — that all poetry in the future will be, or should be, written in such wise as to indicate that its author had read, and profited from reading, this collection. Each poet believes himself original: either he has ventured to realize some hitherto unrealized facet of technical possibility; or he has eclectically fused the aesthetics of his predecessors, believing that his fusion effects something of value for the now and for that vague posterity; or he, to enrich the world, depends solely, and this genre is ubiquitous, on the extraordinary merit of his personality and his view point.

Many of the poems in this book present such difficulties, I am told, as to assure their neglect. Poems which require more than the ordinary curt perusal are, when their author be insufficiently acclaimed to demand a more careful appraisal, destined to remain unread. This in no wise invalidates them as poetry, and even poetry of an high, though a new, order. I shall be tagged 'obscure' when I am but 'difficult.' It has been remarked that an 'obscure' poem is the unsuccessful articulation of a thought, a feeling, or both; and a 'difficult' poem is one which, after a careful and intelligent reading, becomes sufficiently clear.

The poetry which moves, which recreates the mood, the thought, the emotion of the poet is that poetry whose images are most arresting and allied to experience. The logical step between the usual metaphor and the symbol is slight. Believing that the multiplied abstractions found, unhappily, in a Shelley, a Wordsworth, a Swinburne, contribute not at all to the value of their work, I have endeavored to avoid abstractions, have employed them only when, for internal reasons, they supplied necessary

BY HOWARD BLAKE

prose statement, and when they were in context with more concrete terms. For expansion from the particular to the universal, abstractions are imperative. Those words which permit both writer and reader latitude of meaning, such words as 'love,' 'sadness,' even the hackneyed 'beauty,' are employed, when at all, for their general nonsense and personal significance. Frequently the adjective, or word used in that capacity, will seem to have no necessary relation to the noun: in the conviction that all modern poetry should be concise, I have chosen to juxtapose words which, though rhetorically foreign, are, for me, contiguous in association and suggestion. ['Mr All Dithers'] is an example of this treatment. This is not always true: where a word should be stressed, the attendant word has direct bearing on it. In short, quite conscious of the charge that symbols may symbolize for their author alone, I hold a belief in relative catholicity of meaning in the separate word, declare my joining of word to word to be the result of my personal reaction to the subject, supposing myself not so singular as completely to fail in conveyance of my pervasive thought, emotion, or, which may be an union of both, my mood. The notion that a poem is 'successful' only when it approximates an exact reproduction of the author's experience, I would consider absurd. Should a reader succeed in giving to the poem any sequential 'meaning,' the author would be amply justified. Whether or not a poet succeeds in evoking in his reader an experience parallel to his own, rests, ultimately, in the poet's ethos – whether he responds to life as do the many or the few.

The poems are chronologically arranged. The earlier poems, and those toward the middle of the book, have, individually, an unity of thought and treatment; many abstractions are avoided and symbols are employed in their stead. The two last poems might both be entitled Meditations; they have an unity of mood, their thoughts evolve from the mood, and have their sequence in the mood. That a poem should have but one 'idea,' 'thought,' 'meaning,' I would deny: where the mood is the same, there may be as many 'thoughts,' 'meanings,' as the mood, running its verbal course, would spontaneously evoke.

To the percipient, the age is one 'to dizzy and appal.' A poet, in my opinion, has either to join Rome, Marxism, Fascism, any of the creeds, or to remain unanchored, unharbored; to seek truth in experience and contemplation. Unsatisfied with too neat 'parties,' he may strive to transcend them; may try to know himself and his own reactions, believing himself sufficiently like his fellows not wholly to fail in his work of communication. Now joining some party makes possible a poetry simpler than that which is conceived in the open arena, where opinion buffets opinion, where the poet is convinced of the absolute verity of none. In short, to reflect his age, the poet must reflect the obvious and the subtle, the crude and the refined, the present and the past. To many, this last requirement may seem unnecessary; but one who is cognizant of man in time cannot overlook, nor is he ever tempted to forget, the long line of men who, in their separate times and places, have voiced their reactions to worlds dissimilar in the particular though, in the fundamental and more static emotions, analogous.

It is this consciousness of the past which I believe should have important bearing on all poetry. When a poet is read in other than the literature of his contemporaries, it were curious, an intellectual absence of integrity, should this heritage fail, in his work, to manifest itself. The symbolism of such a poet may stem from some work which, in his mind, is related to his own subject and treatment. A line of Webster or Milton might, with some slight change, some slight adaptation, more ably express his meaning than would a line equal in merit of his sole devising. A poem so conceived concentrates a whole vista of time on the experience indited. That the reader should be acquainted with the work memory-paraphrased is, in some instances, necessary; in others, an understanding without this knowledge is attainable. It may, perhaps, seem over-much to require of a reader that he should have read the literature of the past: possibly it is. When the employed key-phrases derive from great works, or works not unread by the literate, requirement of such a knowledge does not present too inordinate a demand. Probably I shall, on some hands, be subjected to the charge of plagiarism: the neo-classical tradition, especially that admirable summary of the view point, Sir Joshua Reynolds' *Discourses*, brilliantly and adequately defends me. This age, in many respects, is not unlike other ages; and I am convinced an awareness of man not alone, but with a long and profound heritage, is necessary to a complete exposition of experience.

The difference between the man who has, in Coleridge's words, 'mistaken an intense desire for natural poetic genius; the love of the arbitrary end for a possession of the peculiar means,' and the man possessed of the 'peculiar means,' is difficult to recognize and impossible to define. It is probable that many current reputations are but the product of such an intense desire: it is possible these poems are. Where true poetry is, there too will be

> *Mists of Envy, fogs of spight,*
> *Twixt mens judgements and her light:*
> *But so much her power may do,*
> *That shee can dissolve them too.*

BOSTON,
6 MAY, 1935